Robert Hall has a Bachelor of Science (Hons) degree in Zoology from the University of Bristol, a Post-Graduate Certification in Education from the University of Cardiff, and a Master of Social Science degree in Russian and East European Studies from the University of Birmingham.

After university, he joined the British army—where he met several animals—and served for 17 years before leaving for the business world in 1992. He has worked in senior managerial roles for a range of commercial organisations, including Jane's Information Group, Barclays, Marsh, BAT and G4S, focusing on resilience, risk and security issues. He served as the head of analysis for the UK's National Criminal Intelligence Service (now the National Crime Agency) from 1997 to 2000, and he was also the managing director of the Global Forum on Law Enforcement and National Security from 2000 to 2002.

His last business appointment was as the cofounder and executive director of Resilience First Ltd, a membership organisation that promotes resilience in commerce.

On stepping down in 2022, he condensed his knowledge of and experience on resilience in a book titled *Building Resilient Futures* which looks at various aspects of human resilience—personal, emotional, organisational, urban, communal and national (Austin Macauley Publishers Ltd, 2023, ISBN: 9781035812622).

Nature's Resilience is a sequel to *Building Resilient Futures* and *The Resilience Mindset: A Philosophical Journey* (Austin Macauley Publishers Ltd, 2025, ISBN: 9781035878284). This book is the last in the series on resilience.

The author's first book, *Soviet Military Art in a Time of Change: Command and Control of the Future Battlefield*, was published at the end of the Cold War (Brassey's, 1991, ISBN: 0080413218). It arose from his work in the UK MoD (Defence Intelligence), where he obtained a defence fellowship.

A historical novel *The Triptych* based on ancestral links was released by Austin Macauley Publishers Ltd in spring 2024.

Robert Hall

NATURE'S RESILIENCE

AUSTIN MACAULEY PUBLISHERS

LONDON · CAMBRIDGE · NEW YORK · SHARJAH

A CIP catalogue record for this title is available from the British Library.

ISBN 9781035878260 (Paperback)
ISBN 9781035878277 (ePub e-book)

www.austinmacauley.com

First Published 2025
Austin Macauley Publishers Ltd®
1 Canada Square
Canary Wharf
London
E14 5AA

I would like to thank my parents, my school teachers and my university lecturers for imbuing me with a deep appreciation of the natural world. My wife, Hilary, has constantly encouraged and shared that appreciation.

I would also like to acknowledge the generous contribution made by Professor Tom Oliver in the Foreword. He kindly provided some textual suggestions that helped with accuracy and clarity.

I would like to thank both Toby Peyton-Jones OBE and Richard Aylard for their words of support by way of the Pre-publication Reviews.

Any errors in the text are entirely the responsibility of the author.

Finally, I would like to identify and praise two publications in particular which have spurred me on to write this book.

The first is a book by Rafe Sagarin called *Learning from the Octopus: How Secrets from Nature Can Help Us Fight Terrorist Attacks, Natural Disasters and Disease* (2012, ISBN: 9780465021833). This was instrumental in shaping my thoughts and gave me the idea of expanding the list of animals and plants to consider under the general resilience label. Rafe was a marine ecologist and environmental policy analyst at the University of Arizona who sadly died after being knocked off his bicycle by a pickup truck near Tucson in 2015.

The second is a more recent publication with a universal message. It is called *Fox and Bear: A Tender Modern Fable About Reversing the Anthropocene* (2022, ISBN: 9780889956469). It is by Miriam Körner, an award-winning author, and is an antidote to the civilisational compulsions that rob human nature of nature. Both as a species and as individuals, Miriam believes we have forgotten who we would be, and what our world would look like, if we lived under the 'benediction of enough'.

Pre-Publication Reviews

Robert Hall, with his killer combination of business and zoology, dives into the natural world for us to show us how much we can learn from our fellow creatures about resilience and how to thrive against the odds. Packed with interest, this book teaches us that lessons from nature are not theoretical, they are hard won, sharpened over millennia on the angle grinder of natural selection. We would do well to listen.

Toby Peyton-Jones OBE

Non-Executive Director for the Department for Education and former Executive Board Member of Siemens UK. BSc in Zoology (University of Nottingham)

Robert Hall's multi-faceted and penetrating analysis of natural resilience is fascinating. He provides a wide range of examples of how it is achieved, and delivers timely warnings about natural limits and the tipping points that face all natural systems. There are many lessons for our human existence, including the difficult choices about where we may need to intervene to maintain and restore equilibrium, and where it might be better to leave nature to take its course, through the complex natural processes that have emerged over millions of years and which we are only beginning to understand.

Richard Aylard

Sustainability Director at Thames Water. BSc in Zoology (University of Reading)

Table of Contents

In the hope of reaching the moon, men fail to see the flowers that blossom at their feet.

−Albert Schweitzer

The imagination of nature is far, far greater than the imagination of man.

−Richard Feynman

More and more I have come to admire resilience. Not the simple resilience of a pillow, whose foam returns over and over to the same shape, but the sinuous tenacity of a tree: finding the light newly blocked on one side, it turns to another. A blind intelligence, true. But out of such persistence arose turtles, rivers, mitochondria, figs—all this resinous, unretractable earth.

−Jane Hirshfield

Preface

Nature's Resilience is about how resilience manifests itself in the natural world and how such biological resilience may help us understand our own human resilience. It is a sequel to *Building Resilient Futures* (2023) in which the author looks exclusively at the human dimension and is a useful primer on resilience, and *The Resilience Mindset: A Philosophical Journey* (2025) in which the author considers the thinking behind the concept of resilience.

The definition of resilience used in these books is 'the ability to anticipate, absorb and adapt to changes because of a shock or stress'.[1] A resilient creature can survive in the face of adversity, recover after confronting that challenge, and then thrive by evolving to deal with the changed set of circumstances.

The ways that biological organisms survive and thrive within a changing world can tell us a lot about ourselves, our behaviours and our approach to problem-solving. We may not be able to learn directly from the pine tree, the bear or the octopus but they can reveal activities, behaviours, even chemicals or genes, that can benefit our world. Moreover, animals and plants have been at the resiliency game for much longer than people and many have thrived through tumultuous, evolutionary times. They can, therefore, provide examples of how nature has solved challenges, and we should be humble enough to take note and reflect.

The solutions can indeed have relevance for our complex and sophisticated range of human activities such as healthcare and well-being, including the sources of valuable drugs that can alleviate human ailments; physical security and national deterrence; crisis management and business continuity; organisational agility and corporate networking. The list is extensive.

The chapters of this book focus on ten profiles of particular organisms (species, genus or group) that have developed their resilient capacities in different ways. The analysis is conducted with the aim of extending our understanding of resilience in a broader context and by so doing provide pointers as to how we might improve and save ourselves from worsening the imbalance between the natural world and the human one. The final chapter looks at the future of resilience for the human race. It explores ways in which we can combine human welfare and national diversity.

The resilience characteristics chosen in the profiles cover aspects of robustness, resistance, recovery, redundancy, agility, adaptation, networking, transformation, preparation, deterrence and regeneration. These are not the only attributes of resilience but are the main ones that are shared throughout the natural (and human) world. They should not be viewed simply as discrete packages operating in silos but as interconnected elements which can be mutually reinforcing. Some may be more prominent in certain species but the majority can be found to varying degrees in most higher animals and more than a few plant species.

The book hopefully sheds some light on the main theme of resilience from the stories of some familiar and not-so-familiar creatures in our diverse global ecosystem. It is not written as an academic book but rather one for the lay reader who wishes to know more about resilience in the natural world and its relevance to our world.

This book is the last in the series on resilience.

Robert Hall
11 February 2025

Foreword

By
Professor Tom Oliver

The age of human exceptionalism is coming to an end. When we pause our hubristic thinking, which is based on assumptions of human superiority, we open ourselves to learning from other species. There appears to be a growing acceptance nowadays, for example, that intelligence can be defined more broadly. Rather than appraising problem-solving behaviours that parallel our own, we now appreciate the distributed intelligence that allows a brainless slime mould to navigate a maze to seek resources. We see intelligence in how tree communities interact with each other through airborne chemicals and via below-ground roots, or in the cognitive abilities of jumping spiders when they strategically plan their attacks.

We can also learn from nature to better design our world better. Biomimicry is the design of materials, structures, and systems modelled on biological entities and processes. When we look to nature with humility, we can learn how to design better aircraft based on the study of bird wings or the movement of sharks; we can learn how to ventilate buildings using less energy by observing how termites build their nests;

we can develop new lightweight materials for vehicles by studying the bodies of creatures such as mantis shrimps.

Now it is time to learn lessons from nature about resilience. This delightful book draws on diverse examples from butterflies to beavers, and limpets to lodgepole pines, in order to understand how species resist, recover and transform in the face of environmental stress. It is certainly timely for us humans to better learn some of these skills since we are causing unprecedented transformation of our global environment—dramatically changing the composition of our atmosphere, soils, freshwaters and oceans.

We are impacting living ecosystems from coral reefs to tropical rainforests and, in some cases, we are even risking their collapse. This rapid global environmental change increasingly presents humanity with serious risks, from heatwaves and toxic smog to multiple breadbasket failures and disease pandemics. The mitigation of damage to nature and reducing greenhouse gas emissions and slowing biodiversity loss, for example, are still more essential than ever, but there is also a rapidly growing need to plan for tough times ahead.

Understanding risk and resilience for human societies is becoming increasingly important. This focus on humans should not come at the expense of protecting other species of course and, in fact, we can learn many lessons on resilience by studying them. If myopic and hubristic (anthropocentric) thinking got us into this mess, it might just be that a new more-than-human perspective will help get us out of it.

Tom Oliver is Research Dean for Environment and Professor of Applied Ecology at the School of Biological Sciences at the University of Reading.

His book The Self Delusion *explores how people, animals, plants and the planet we live on are all intimately connected—and why that matters.[2] He is an advisor to the UK government, the Office for Environmental Protection, and the European Commission on environmental risks and an External Advisory Board member for the Leverhulme Centre for Anthropocene Biodiversity.*

Introduction

Resilience is a life-sustaining characteristic. It is comparable to eating and breathing in animals or photosynthesis and transpiration in plants. It allows all creatures not just to survive as individual organisms at the moment but also to thrive as species in a world of challenges and constant change. It gives the sentient or insentient the impetus to rise above environmental pressures and provides the evolutionary motive to continue and adapt both individually and collectively in our common biosphere.

The significance of resilience in the natural world has largely gone unreported until the last half century when it became a dedicated subject in the field of ecology and more recently in the human condition. Today, it is hard to read or hear commentary about people, organisations, communities or countries, and their associated activities, without resilience becoming part of the conversational vocabulary. The global concerns about environmental degradation and climate change have reinvigorated the lexicon.

In fact, resilience is not a new word. It was introduced into the English language in the early seventeenth century from the Latin verb *resilire* meaning to rebound or recoil. The base of *resilire* is *salire*, a verb meaning 'to leap' which is symbolic. Resilience came into prominence in the early nineteenth century in the world of engineering and physics where it was (and continues to be) seen as the ability of a material to absorb energy such as from a blow or distortion, and release that energy as it returns to its original shape. In the world of engineers, resilience is about resistance and recovery.

For biologists and ecologists studying the natural world, resilience has come to mean much more. It is the ability to absorb external shocks or stresses as well as to change or adapt to a new set of life-giving experiences—that 'leap' of earlier. This may involve simply learning from experience and modifying behaviour but it can require some restructuring of shape or function. For ecological resilience, it may be a case of maintaining the same function but undergoing internal reorganisation or even more radical transformation. In essence, resilience is about surviving and thriving in response to change.[3] It is certainly not an attribute confined to humans.

Biological life has proved to be remarkably resilient over aeons. For over three billion years, life on Earth has survived and thrived in the face of seismic shocks and stresses. It has evolved, adapted and mutated into a multitude of species that have occupied a diverse array of habitats, filling almost every niche on the planet. At the same time, many species have been unable to cope with their new environments and become extinct. Many more will inevitably fall by the wayside in our continuing planetary journey; that is an unavoidable but necessary part of evolution.

Yet enough plants and animals have survived five mass extinctions on Earth to allow life to prosper. A sixth mass extinction is foretold by some—the United Nations predicts one million plants and animals, or three-quarters of all species, will be extinct by 2039[4]—but it is reasonable and hopeful to assume, if only from historical precedence, that life will continue in some form or other. It was Charles Darwin who recognised such extinctions as the motor of evolution. Yet arresting and reversing the decline in biodiversity— 'bending the curve'—requires concerted, global action.[5]

That reasonable assumption should not, however, be taken for granted; it cannot be a foregone conclusion. Much needs to change if hope for planetary survival and biological diversity is to be assured. Diversity gives species the opportunities to exploit changing environments and find new solutions for survival; the less diversity there is, the fewer those opportunities. This can be quantified in monetary terms. According to the World Economic Forum, more than half the world's GDP ($44 trillion) is at risk of disruption due to nature's loss.[6]

All sectors, from fishing and agriculture to construction and pharmaceuticals, have a significant interest in protecting nature due to the huge value that they derive from natural capital. The Kunming-Montreal Global Biodiversity Framework, arising from the United Nations Fifteenth Conference of the Parties, stated one of its goals would be: 'The integrity, connectivity and resilience of all ecosystems are maintained, enhanced or restored, substantially increasing the area of natural ecosystems by 2050.'[7]

Whether people will be part of the post-Anthropocene epoch is a separate question. We have certainly been successful so far, with eight billion people currently inhabiting the earth while the number is expected to reach ten billion by the end of this century. Humans now dominate the planet to such an extent that together we weigh more than ten times that of all the wild animals on the land combined: 390 million tonnes versus 22 million tonnes, respectively. [8] Success in numbers has brought about its own problems, however, one of which is the need for around 1.8 earth equivalents to sustain the human population if we continue to consume the world's resources at the present rate.[9]

Sustainability, in contrast to resilience, can be seen as the capacity of a whole system or sub-system to endure over the long term. In ecology, sustainability describes how biological systems can remain diverse and productive over time. Long-lived healthy wetlands and mixed-leaf deciduous forests are examples of sustainable ecosystems. For people, sustainability is the potential for long-term maintenance of the global population and its overall well-being, albeit with environmental, economic and social considerations. A sustainable human community should be able to maintain a prolonged quality of life for its inhabitants and the natural environment on which is depends from external pressures and from internal influences.

In a sustainable community, the pressures and influences are usually incremental and system-wide whereas a resilient community must cope in the face of adversity and recover after confronting a specific and short-term threat or danger. An integral part of resilience is the ability to adapt and change. People have been good at adapting and learning in the face of shocks and stresses, so much so that the *status quo ante* is often replaced with a new condition or set of behaviours that may themselves generate whole new challenges. This is evolution—and resilience—at work.

While biological systems can be both sustainable and resilient, a resilient system may not necessarily be sustainable. Take the example of the lodgepole pine (*Pinus contorta*) in the USA. (See *Chapter 2*.) The tree produces seeds which are resilient to the heat from a forest fire and allow regrowth after any fire. However, if the frequency of the fires becomes so great that it prevents the seedlings from reaching maturity and producing their own seeds then the species cannot regenerate and will die.

It could be argued that the threshold for resilience in this circumstance has been surpassed but if sufficient numbers of the total tree population do survive, sustainability can be maintained. It is not the only species to be facing such dilemmas. With climate change, sustainability is a real and present feature for many animals and plants.

The prominence of the work on ecological resilience owes much to a US-Canadian academic, Crawford Stanley Holling.[10] He believed that the ability of natural systems to persist in the face of major changes suggested that they have a high capacity to absorb change without dramatically altering. But Holling acknowledged that this resilient character has its limits or tipping points and when these limits are exceeded the ecosystem could rapidly change to another condition. Too much disturbance could lead to systemic degeneration but, at the same time, periodic disturbance within limits could also contribute to an ecosystem's transformation to a more diverse and more dynamic, vibrant condition. The inability to adapt to a major event could push a society or community to utilise new and more sophisticated forms of adaptation, or become extinct.

Holling argued that paradoxically, instability can induce resilience as a way of achieving equilibrium (homeostasis).[11] Ecosystems, like all open systems, tend towards equilibrium in order to maintain their integrity. He concluded that an ecological system can be very resilient and still fluctuate greatly, provided it can absorb shocks without major loss of form and function. Tropical rain forests and mangrove swamps are examples of systems which can prevail through periodic droughts or torrential storms providing global temperatures do not exceed certain levels. Beyond the tipping point, they may become savanna or sand, respectively.

Other ecologists have extensively researched the robustness of ecosystems, utilising the general systems principle that they would tend to develop equilibrium.[12,13] They have viewed stress as the motor of homeostasis in which the forces applied to the ecosystem would induce changes that tended to preserve its overall stability. This idea has since been questioned by others who have seen resilience as a catch-all term for the function and behaviour of individual organisms. Some scientists have argued that this does not necessarily add up to stability but can denote constant change.[14] Hence, resilience could be a mark of an ecosystem's ability to keep adapting, not its propensity to keep returning to any given equilibrium. This has been referred to as 'transformational resilience'.

Regardless of whether one accepts or rejects that these ideas can be transferred from ecology to disaster risk reduction, there is no doubt that Holling and the other ecologists made a significant contribution when they began to utilise adaptive management in resilience studies. Recent work has extended this concept to adaptive governance or adaptive capacity, namely adaptive co-management as a continuous problem-solving process.

As a result of this work, resilience came to be seen as the ability of habitats to adapt to shocks and stresses over any timeframe. Such perturbations could include natural events such as fires, floods and hurricanes, as well as human activities such as deforestation, fracking, pesticide spraying and even the introduction of exotic plant or animal species. Unlike mechanical resilience, the behaviour of ecosystems under constant change is focused on durability and adaptability.

An initial focus on the stability of processes in ecosystems and the speed with which they return to an equilibrium state following disturbance (the process of 'recovery' in engineering resilience) has gradually been replaced by a broader concept of ecological resilience. [15] This shift recognises multiple stable states and the ability of systems to resist 'regime shifts' and thereby to maintain functions, potentially through internal reorganisation. [16] Tom Oliver et al make the case that internal reorganisation, such as species turnover in the face of climate change, allows the resilience of function such as pollination. The ecological resilience literature is somewhat vague with regards to what aspects of the system should be resistant in the face of an environmental perturbation.

Within reasonable bounds, forests, for example, can adapt to a constantly changing environment through the mix of tree species and the density of leaf cover. The notion of sustainable ecosystems can also be seen in animal societies like ant and bee colonies. In such nests, insects can recover from considerable disruption by collaboratively working together to enact rapid repairs, irrespective of the cause of that disruption. In fact, biological organisms have over millennia been able to respond to significant change without planning, predicting or tying their responses to complex threats. They simply adapt to solve the challenges they continually face. This is a lesson for human resilience.

All species coexist in and among the natural world. We share common land, sea and air. Sometimes, it seems as if we are too often in conflict with nature, or at the very least try to tame it for our own purposes. That approach may have been acceptable in the early days of man's evolution but in the modern era there is the danger that we so unbalance our relationship with nature by our personal requirements and commercial (mis)management that the sixth extinction is brought about sooner rather than later. As the tipping point is not a firm red line but a gradual and messy degradation then, like the frog in the pot of slowly boiling water, the dangers may be recognised too late to correct the mistakes. As we are finding with climate change, getting enough people to change their behaviours to mitigate the effects and adapt to the consequences are major challenges in what is a shortening time horizon.

In her book *Sacred Nature* (2022), Karen Armstrong argues that if we want to avert environmental catastrophe, it is not enough to change our behaviour or mindset: we need to learn to think and feel differently about the natural world.[17] Besides any spiritual or psychological refocusing, there is the very real practical one of how to prepare for inevitable and wide-scale change in our relationship with the natural world. Resilience is key to this.

Efforts to increase food production have so far focused, for example, on maximising control and productivity while giving insufficient attention to crop and land-use resilience which together aim to reduce food-supply vulnerability. Hence, there is a need for stronger adoption of resilience thinking in bio-based production systems i.e. socio-ecological systems that combine social organisation, human technology, biological processes and ecological systems and their services in the production of food, fibre or biomass.[18]

Preparedness is a major tenet of resilience. It is about not just reducing the boiling water in the pan (in the frog analogy) but also finding ways that others in the natural world have overcome the dangers and difficulties—in advance. It is perhaps not surprising that nature has found many ways to solve survival problems without getting scolded. While bacteria are known to survive and thrive in undersea thermal plumes registering at hundreds of degrees centigrade, the broader issue is how to adapt to changing environments by preparing responses and shielding mechanisms. (See *Chapter 4*.)

Rather than dealing with high temperatures, take the opposite example of cold. Plants and animals do not fight winter—they prepare and adapt. They have three main options: they can migrate to warmer climes, they can hibernate, or they can adapt by developing extra insulation. For those who choose to hibernate, such as bats, hedgehogs, and bears, they perform extraordinary feats of transformation to get through the harsh times. Many shut down their metabolisms to stretch scant resources and may vanish from sight.

Adaptation, on the other hand, is about accepting the dangers and developing techniques to live with the consequences. Growing a winter coat is crucial for an Arctic animal such as the musk ox (*Ovibos moschatus*). Besides laying down a good layer of body fat, it grows an extra inner coat (qiviut) to complement the outer guard hairs which can be as long as 60 cm: other adaptations include a barrel-shaped body and short legs which reduce the ratio of body mass to surface area and thereby minimise heat loss.

At the human level, people can mitigate the worst effects of climate change by trying to reduce the levels of carbon dioxide in the air. We also need to adapt to the existing and accumulating carbon dioxide levels by modifying our approaches and behaviours towards burning fossil fuels. We need to look, for instance, at nature-based solutions (NbS) as well as gain inspiration from creatures that illustrate a high degree of energy efficiency in their various habitats. (See *Chapter 10*.)

One challenge behind NbS and conservation is the measurement of the economic value that they bring. With a multitude of factors, often behind an ill-defined concept, it is hard to present robust assessments. According to Metrick and Weitzman, the value to humans of nature conservation has two sources. [19] The first is the direct utility they provide humanity, so-called 'ecosystem services'. These vary from the aesthetic pleasure that plants provide to those visiting a garden to the more prosaic such as pollinators fertilising crops or earthworms keeping the soil healthy.

The other sources come from an indirect value on biodiversity. This reflects the significance of the genetic information of species and their place in the overall catalogue of the millions of species: it is essentially a cost-benefit analysis. Certain 'keystone' species may be worth preserving over others in any resource-constrained 'ark'—the cited authors use the allegory of Noah's Ark to reflect their deliberations. Trying to keep two species alive, and failing, could mean losing everything. Preventing just one type of animal from going extinct preserves not only what is distinct about that animal but everything it shares genetically with every other animal as well. The utility of each species can therefore be measured as a combination of economic, recreational and scientific reactions.

The challenge of measuring resilience in animals and plants is not dissimilar to that in human populations. The sources, sometimes referred to as 'capitals', involve social, physical, natural and economic factors. An alternative is to look at processes, place, preparation and performance in a maturity model. While absolute quantities in all these factors are difficult to identify and attribute, whether for corporations or cities, various systems have been proposed to provide a more qualitative judgement.

One step to assessing human resilience is through the process of benchmarking. This is a comparative measure rather than an absolute one, often pitting departments (internal benchmarking) or entire organisations (external benchmarking) against one another in functional or competitive ways. Efforts here should be proportional to the dangers faced and the sophistication of the organisation under the spotlight.

Beyond the complexity and innovations of human society, and the challenges of conserving biodiversity, it is possible to find novel ways to adapt to a changing planet. As plants and animals have been doing this for time immemorial, we can and should study and learn from their solutions. They give us hope that there are answers out there that may help with our current plight of climate change, societal dislocation and economic distress. We should not be too proud or hubristic to acknowledge that other forms of life have incorporated resilience into their lives much better than we have.

We begin with an animal that is all around us but hardly ever noticed, the so-called elephant in the room but on a much, much smaller scale. It is the tardigrade, a creature which introduces a fundamental and essential feature of resilience, namely robustness.

Chapter 1
Robustness and the Tardigrade

It is the diversity that makes any natural system robust.
–Marilynne Robinson

We commonly associate robustness with that positive attribute or attitude in ourselves which helps us overcome challenges by showing characteristics such as durability, stoicism, perseverance, toughness, resolve, endurance and hardiness. By being robust, we battle on, refuse to give up and show true grit when facing problems or crises. It can be summarised by the rather basic question: How much can you take before you fall down? Yet these descriptions are not just human characteristics. Nearly every biological species or system displays a degree of what we refer to as robustness in the face of quotidian turmoil, serial disruption or pernicious change. To do otherwise and fail in that pursuit means the species is unlikely to 'survive and thrive'—the essence of resilience—and inextricably lead to an evolutionary dead end.

When examining robustness alongside resilience, it is important to be clear as the meaning of words matters. A robust species or system can withstand external shocks and stresses: robustness refers to strength and effectiveness in adverse conditions. A complex network can be robust if it keeps its basic functionality even when some of its components fail. The important point is that robustness means there is minimal impact or change despite external pressures. A bird's nest is robust if it can withstand the wind and rain and still host the chicks. In infrastructural terms, a bridge is robust if it can withstand the regular traffic flow under all weathers without deforming.

Similarly, a person is robust if he or she can continue with a project even if the working conditions are harsh and unfavourable. Robustness generally occurs prior to resilience—protection first, then recovery. As we shall see later, the way in which robustness plays a role in the protection of a biological species or system is generally distinct from the manner in which resilience plays a role in the recovery of the system.

More than robustness is needed if a species or system is to be resilient. A resilient species or person has the ability not just to be robust but also to bounce back after a setback and adapt to a new environment. It can be summarised by the alternative basic question: How long do you take to stand up again after you fall down? While the individual may well be affected by a perturbation, the ability and strength to cope, recover and adapt afterwards are what makes resilience. This adaptation will involve a degree of change, even transformation, because only through change will the species or system be better prepared for further perturbations and evolution. The element of change is what distinguishes robustness from resilience.

A surviving and thriving biological community should be able to ensure that its structure and organisation are sufficiently robust and resilient not only to mitigate harm to the community but also to allow the community to grow and develop. This means that there is an uneasy relationship and mutuality between robustness and resilience. The two act in concert but place different requirements on the species or system. They may also have different time windows of observation so that what looks like resistance at a coarser scale may actually be a very rapid recovery. There may even be occasions for a trade-off whereby greater robustness requires less resilience or vice versa.

The polar bear (*Ursus maritimus*), for example, may be robust to cold climates but less resilient to warming seas. As we shall see in *Chapter 5*, the common octopus (*Octopus vulgaris*) may be resilient to habitat change but less robust to close interactions through commercial farming. Clearly, an engineer's view of robustness, say in a physical infrastructure, is not what a biologist would look for, say in an animal or plant community. However, one can inform and reinforce the other.

The tardigrade (*Tardigrada*) is a prime example of robustness in the animal kingdom. This is a microorganism that is ubiquitous but is probably one that most people are unaware of or would even recognise. It holds secrets that engineers and biologists alike would dearly like to unlock.

***

Tardigrades, otherwise known as water bears or moss piglets, are a group of eight-legged, segmented, microscopic animals, of which there are over 1,200 known species. They are on average about half a millimetre long when fully grown—about the size of the full stop at the end of this sentence. The largest adults may reach a body length of 1.2 mm. They are short and stubby with four pairs of legs, each ending in claws or suction discs. The hindmost legs point backwards in a configuration unlike that of any other animal. These rear legs are used for grasping and slow-motion acrobatics rather than for walking.

The animals can usually be found in mosses and lichens—hence, their common name—and feed on plant cells, algae and small invertebrates. They are essentially aquatic animals that are surrounded by a layer of water which enables them to sustain their daily life.

Tardigrades are encased in a rugged but flexible cuticle that must be shed as the organism grows, similar to spiders, beetles and other arthropods. Tardigrades are divided into two classes, *Eutardigrada* and *Heterotardigrada*. As a rule, the members of the former have a naked or smooth cuticle without plates whereas the latter boasts a cuticle armoured with plates. The average lifespan of an active tardigrade rarely extends more than a few months.

Tardigrades have been found in diverse regions of the Earth's biosphere from mountain tops, the deep sea and tropical rainforests, to even the Antarctic. This is because they can withstand temperatures close to absolute zero (-273°C) while others can withstand temperatures up to 150°C for several minutes, as well as pressures about six times greater than those found in the deepest ocean trenches, ionising radiation at doses hundreds of times higher than the lethal dose for a person, and even the vacuum of outer space.

However, extreme survival applies only to some species of terrestrial tardigrades. Marine and aquatic tardigrades did not evolve these characteristics because their environments are relatively stable. It appears that the extreme survival adaptations have been selected in direct response to rapidly changing terrestrial micro-environments of damp flora that are subject to rapid drying and severe weather.

Tardigrades are therefore among the most robust animals known, with individual species able to survive extreme conditions, not just extreme temperatures and pressures but also air deprivation, dehydration and starvation—dangers that would quickly kill most other known forms of life. In fact, tardigrades have survived all five mass extinctions on Earth since the group evolved about half a billion years ago.

The creatures exhibit distinctly different responses to different sources of stress. Under severe drought or cold, they change into what are called 'tuns', but there are different forms depending on the environmental assaults. When the environment becomes extremely dry (anhydrobiosis), a desiccated, shrivelled tun forms as the animal retracts its legs and head and curls into a ball—about one-third of its original size—which minimises its surface area. When nearly all its internal water has been surrendered, the tardigrade is in a state of suspended animation (cryptobiosis).[20]

It is almost as if the animal preserves itself by becoming a powder comprised of the basic ingredients of life. While in this state, metabolism drops to less than 0.01% of normal, and water content can drop to 1% of normal. The animals can go without food or water for several years or even decades in exceptional cases, only to later rehydrate, forage and reproduce. To prevent cell death, it appears that some tardigrades synthesise trehalose, a sugar substitute for water, so body structure and cell membranes remain intact.[21] When rehydrated by dew, rain or melting snow, tardigrades can return to their active state within a few minutes or just a few hours.

A tardigrade tun. This forms during severe drought or cold. A tardigrade can stay in a tun state for decades. Credit: Shutterstock

With low temperatures (cryobiosis) on the other hand, it seems likely that survival is conferred by the release or synthesis of cryoprotectants which slow the freezing process and allow an orderly transition into a suspended state that will facilitate subsequent revival by thawing. There is no tun formation. Induced proteins appear to disrupt ice crystallisation. If this did not occur, the cells of the tardigrade would rupture as ice formed and expanded. These survival attributes are, in fact, quite suitable for an organism that makes its home in mosses and lichens which provide it with a thin layer of environmental protection.

When there is a lack or low levels of oxygen (anoxybiosis) or excessive concentrations of gases such as carbon dioxide or sulphur dioxide, tardigrades become turgid and elongated. They take on the appearance of a 'Michelin Man' until the environment returns to normal.[22] The increased surface area presented will help capture what little oxygen is around. Again, there is no tun formation. Some tardigrades exhibit strikingly effective osmoregulation, maintaining stasis of their metabolism in the face of steep osmotic gradients. Some others escape via the formation of a tun that is impervious to osmotic transfer.

Surviving intense radiation suggests an especially effective DNA repair system in an active organism. The robustness of one *Eutardigrada* species (*Ramazzottius varieornatus*) is in part due to a unique protein in its body called Dsup (damage suppressor) that protects the DNA from being harmed by things like ionising radiation which is present in soil, water and vegetation.[23] The same mechanism is also thought to protect the tardigrade from the solar radiation, severely low temperatures and the vacuum of space. Cryobiotic tardigrades returning to Earth on a spacecraft following experimental exposure, and then rehydrated, were able to move, eat, grow and reproduce. The ability to do this may have transferrable lessons.

Another interesting resilience characteristic is the tardigrade's ability to reproduce quickly—always a good survive-and-thrive technique, especially if the normal life cycle is short. Many tardigrades living in moss, lichen and leaf litter can produce eggs without mating (parthenogenetic) and in a few cases are able to self-fertilise (hermaphroditic). In some species, males deposit sperm inside the cuticle of a moulting, egg-carrying female during an hour-long mating activity. Some females shed their cuticle and then lay their eggs inside to be fertilised later by males.

Eggs take around 40 days to hatch, or as long as 90 days if they have been in a desiccated state. A lone tardigrade—active, tun or egg—picked up by the wind may be able to establish a population where it lands if the habitat is suitable. In the tun state, they are barely distinguishable from dust particles.

The rapid reproductive rate gives the tardigrade an evolutionary and resilience advantage as it can recover its population quickly and extensively when threatened. In population biology, there is the theory of 'r' (for rate) and 'K' (for the German *Kapazitätsgrenze* or capacity limit). [24] Although r/K selection theory has been modified over time, the concept was one of the first predictive models for evolution. R-strategists are generalists and secure their perpetuation through fast reproduction in a short time.

The tardigrade is an example of an organism that exhibits r-selected traits; others include ants, rats and frogs. They are generally of small body size, have early maturity, short generation time, and the ability to disperse offspring widely.

Here, there is little advantage in specialisation that permits successful competition with other organisms because the environment is likely to change again.

In summary, we witness in tardigrades different responses to environmental extremes: the passive response of dormancy in the form of cryptobiosis, counterbalanced by the hyperactive responses of impressive DNA repair, and high-performance osmoregulation. As practitioners of adaptive evolution, tardigrades are virtuosos. They improvise, adapt and overcome the challenges in their environment. This must make them a resilient species.

***

Some experts consider tardigrades as belonging to an elite category of animals known as extremophiles, namely those that can survive environments that most others cannot. However, others do not consider them extremophilic because they are not adapted to exploit these conditions, only equipped to endure them. This means that their chances of dying increase the longer they are exposed to extreme environments, whereas true extremophiles thrive in a physically or geochemically extreme environment that would harm most other organisms.

At the top end of the temperature-survivable range, for example, is a microbe called *Methanopyrus kandleri*. This is a heat- and salt-loving species of single-celled *Archaea* that makes its home on the chimney walls of hydrothermal vents (smokers). It harvests energy from hydrogen gas and releases methane, a process known as methanogenesis. It is this process that gives the microbe its generic name which translates as 'methane fire'.

In the laboratory, its cells can even divide at 122°C, the highest temperature known to be compatible with microbial growth, though it grows best at 98°C. According to one report, 40% of a tested species of *Bacillus* bacteria from soil in Morocco survived in a dried spore stage after being heated to temperatures of 420°C.[25]

At the opposite end of the temperature spectrum, the tardigrade is also not the only animal or plant to have biological mechanisms that allow it to withstand cold and for prolonged periods. As we shall see, the ability is widespread and can persist for millennia.

In the case of trees, which clearly cannot hibernate or migrate, they have bark around their trunks which provides insulation against freezing and cracking during the winter. Broadleaf, deciduous trees lose their leaves in the winter to reduce water loss. Most needle-leaved trees, the conifers, retain needles all year round—with exceptions such as larch (*Larix*) and bald cypress (*Taxodium distichum*)—only losing older, damaged needles. Needles are better at retaining water than broad leaves thanks to their small surface area and a waxy outer coating that limits water loss to transpiration, the evaporation of water from leaves.

Trees and some plants begin to prepare for an oncoming winter in late summer as daylight hours decline, entering a dormant state and reaching their adapted tolerance by mid-winter. Through a combination of cellular changes that involve shrinkage, dehydration and sugar concentration, the cells harden and become glasslike. This helps prevent freezing and damage to living cells. Lichens, for example, grow very slowly and can withstand cold temperatures, including surviving beneath snow.

Animals such as the polar bear (*Ursus maritimus*), Arctic char (*Salvelinus alpinus*) and Arctic fox (*Vulpes lagopus*), as well as wolves, penguins, seals and whales, all have adaptations like fur or fat to help withstand low temperatures. At really low temperatures, other techniques are necessary such as the use of some form of anti-freeze (cryoprotectant). When deploying cryoprotectants, insects often use sugars or polyols: one species that uses cryoprotectants is a wasp (*Polistes exclamans*). Cold-adapted Arctic frogs, such as the wood frog (*Lithobates sylvaticus*), and some other ectotherms in polar and subpolar regions naturally produce glucose as a cryoprotectant, but the southern brown tree frog (*Litoria ewingii*) and Arctic salamander (*Salamandrella keyserlingii*) create glycerol in their livers to reduce ice formation.

Wood frogs can remain frozen solid for up to eight months each year as they remain out of water but under the snow. In these amphibians, massive amounts of glucose are released by the liver and a special form of insulin allows for this extra glucose to enter every cell. Hibernating wood frogs can tolerate blood sugar levels 100 times higher than normal without the damage experienced by human diabetics when their blood sugar is only 2–10 times above normal. When the frog rewarms during spring, the extra glucose is rapidly eliminated but remains stored in the animal's body.[26] The process allows the frogs to become active and breed very early in spring and become frogs that hibernate under water.

Understanding how frogs can do this might provide valuable knowledge to help in the management of high blood sugar in people with diabetes. Also, the wood frog's ability to withstand freezing may help explain how human organs used for transplants could be frozen and thawed without damage. This would increase the allowable time between removing an organ from a donor and implanting it within the recipient, which could in turn make many more transplants possible. Researchers are also interested in how the wood frog's body can stop blood circulation and start it again many months later without blood clots or other injuries. Understanding this mechanism could be valuable for treating people after their blood flow is temporarily halted by heart attack or stroke.[27]

The tardigrade's ability to survive across a wide range of temperature extremes is due to its unique biological features. An understanding of these processes could greatly benefit humankind in its efforts to preserve life in extremely cold or dry climates and in long-term space travel. Robustness to ionising radiation and the ability to undertake DNA repair are also assets that space travellers would value. The ability of the tardigrade to enter suspended animation (cryptobiosis) to endure freezing or desiccating environments is a capability that could be part of future food and agricultural science (cryopreservation) as well as one for prolonging human tissue or even life itself for those looking for such solutions.

Cryptobiosis extends to other species. Spectacular examples of long-term cryptobiosis include a *Bacillus* spore that had been preserved in the abdomen of bees buried in amber for 25–40 million years.[28] A 1,300-year-old lotus seed (*Nelumbo nucifera*) found in an ancient lake was subsequently able to germinate.[29]

An announcement that a hitherto unknown species of nematode worm (*Panagrolaimus kolymaensis*) has been awoken after lying dormant for 46,000 years in the Siberian

41

permafrost demonstrates that a species is capable not merely of surviving in stasis but also of doing so over geological time (in this case since the late Pleistocene period). [30] This discovery raises questions about our definition of what it is to be alive. If bacteria and worms can be reactivated, there is the possibility that agents harmful to people might also emerge from a thawing permafrost.

The pursuit of cryonics—the storage of human tissue at very low temperatures with the speculative hope that resurrection may be possible in the future—is viewed with scepticism by many scientists. Cryopreservation in humans with regards to infertility, however, is already a common feature and involves the preservation of embryos, sperm or oocytes via freezing. Cryopreservation has its dangers though. Excessively rapid cooling kills cells by intracellular ice formation while excessively slow cooling kills cells by either electrolyte toxicity or mechanical crushing. During slow cooling, ice forms extracellularly, causing water to leave cells osmotically thereby dehydrating them.[31]

Intracellular ice can be much more damaging than extracellular ice. Cryoprotectants, such as dimethyl sulfoxide and glycerol, can be used to protect cells from freezing. Some cryobiologists are seeking mixtures of cryoprotectants for full vitrification (zero-ice formation) in the preservation of cells, tissues and organs. Vitrification methods pose a challenge to the search for cryoprotectant mixtures that can minimise toxicity.

The tardigrade's robustness to extreme temperatures, and the types of cryoprotectants it deploys, could offer new ways forward for cryobiologists.

People are less tolerant of low temperatures, needing to keep the core body temperature at around 37°C. Hypothermia usually sets in when the body temperature goes below 35°C. Guðlaugur Friðþórsson, an Icelandic fisherman, survived for six hours in 5°C cold water after his fishing vessel capsized in March 1984. After swimming to land, he trekked for another three hours across lava fields in bare feet to reach a town for help in freezing conditions. Guðlaugur's body temperature was below 34°C yet he showed almost no symptoms of hypothermia or vasodilation, only of dehydration.

In subsequent medical trials, the 23-year-old Icelander showed phenomenal robustness to endure the cold. He was probably saved by the fact that at 6'4" in height and weighing 275lbs he had a BMI in excess of 30, so would have had a good layer of internal fat. (Guðlaugur's exploits are portrayed in the 2012 film *The Deep*.)

There are many other examples of human robustness in the face of extreme conditions. Sir Ernest Shackleton's exploits in the Endurance expedition to Antarctica in 1914–16 are but one. Despite losing his ship to the pack ice, Shackleton managed to save his crew of 27 by sailing for 16 days in a small boat across 800 miles of the Southern Ocean in freezing conditions. He and two others then had to trek across a snow-covered mountain before reaching help. Shackleton's experience of the region probably imbued him with the robustness to survive the ordeal.

Robustness in more routine, everyday situations is still required for resilience. More robust crisis-management processes and capabilities are commonly called for by business organisations in today's volatile and turbulent world.

More robust regulation of financial services or trading standards are other demands. When it comes to the young or inexperienced, more robust teaching to instil stronger personal characteristics is said by some to be needed to counter the increase in anxiety and decline in mental health; others would dispute this assertion.

Character building is certainly a feature of military training which tries to toughen up soldiers, sailors and aircrew in readiness for testing and dangerous situations. Ultimately, it forms a positive belief system and a sense of individual capability and self-awareness. It is a combination of nature and nurture, like resilience in general.

Robustness can be improved with experience of life's ups and downs. Practice is perhaps the best form of training. However, it naturally takes time and has the potential for several missed steps. It should not be just considered in the context of extremes but also in daily experience and as part of being more resilient to life's challenges. It requires a form of metaphysical armour or 'hard' skills to protect the inner 'soft' skills from being overwhelmed and unable to function. This is where the tardigrade cannot help.

Some argue that it may be possible to be 'robust yet fragile', a term coined by scientist John Doyle. [32] At the same time as complex systems are resilient in the face of anticipated dangers, they can be highly susceptible to unanticipated dangers. A popular case study for complex networks, as exemplified by Doyle, has been the internet with a major issue being the extent to which its design and evolution have made it robust yet fragile. It may be unaffected by random component failures but it is vulnerable to targeted attacks on its key nodes. As the complexity of such systems grows, both the sources and severity of possible disruptions increase, even as the size required for potential triggering events decreases. It can take only a tiny event, at the wrong place or at the wrong time, to spark a calamity—the so-called beating of the butterfly wings syndrome (the Lorenz concept) as part of chaos theory.[33]

In his book (2012) of the same name, Nassim Taleb introduces the term 'antifragile'.[34] Most people would say that the opposite of fragility is robustness. Yet Taleb believes that there is a step beyond robustness, namely antifragility when something becomes stronger when it is damaged like the mythical Hydra growing two heads when one is cut off. He thinks antifragility is necessary if we are to thrive and claims that antifragility goes beyond resilience or robustness—the resilient resists shocks and stays the same, and the antifragile gets better. Not all agree with Taleb's idea.

The simple tardigrade does show that is necessary to be robust to more than one challenge or extreme, sometimes concurrently. It is no good to be robust to cold but succumb to heat; that is not being truly resilient. When nature can present unexpected challenges, it pays to be flexible and dynamic. This is also true for humans. People tend to focus on the latest threat or hazard and think that a sound, robust response to one risk is all that is needed, and resilience will automatically spill over into other counter-threat domains.

In the official inquiry report on the failings around the Manchester Arena bombing in 2017, for instance, it has been acknowledged that the UK's Security Service (MI5) focused too much on one threat (Syrian returnees) at the expense of another (Libyan returnees).[35] Yet it is fair to say that robustness to flooding, for example, has few similarities to robustness to a cyber-attack. This notwithstanding, we need to consider both at the same time in terms of general preparation for disruption, having back-ups or workarounds, having clean-up remedies, etc, all difficult tasks especially when resources are limited. Some of the counter-measures may be generic: recovery sites and adequate reserves are usually common features.

The other feature of the tardigrade worthy of comparison, and with relevance elsewhere, is its reproductive capacity. In contrast to r-strategists like the tardigrade, K-strategists are specialists. They are slow at reproducing with high investment in a small number of singular offspring so are more likely to survive; they are heavily adapted to their environment. Species that exhibit K-selected traits include gorillas, eagles, whales…and humans.

Many organisms fit into both r- and K-categories and adopt different strategies depending on local conditions at any one time. Some researchers believe that an organism capable of alternating between the two strategies may be the most successful organism in the long term because of its ability to adapt and survive under a much broader range of conditions. Some reptiles such as sea turtles display both r- and K-traits, for example. Although sea turtles are large organisms with long lifespans on reaching adulthood, they produce large numbers of unnurtured offspring.

When a particular biome flourishes and is stable, K-strategists tend to predominate. However, when that biome changes, becomes unstable or is disrupted, r-strategists come to the fore and K-strategists weaken. Interestingly, scientists have found that animals that have fast lives with strategies are more resilient to human-driven changes in land use than those with K-strategies.[36]

People have built a heavily weighted K-strategy society so when disruption hits, they are hard-pressed to adapt quickly. tardigrades, on the other hand, have little social order by evolving unique biological processes that allow them to be as populous and dispersed as humans. The tardigrade has accepted the trade-off here and may be around much longer than people as a result.

The other group of r-strategy creatures worthy of note under the heading of robustness (see also *Chapter 2* on Resistance) is the microorganisms like viruses and bacteria. As has already been noted, some microbes can live for long periods in hostile environments. Once inside a suitable host, they can reproduce at prodigious rates and spell disaster when their toxins overwhelm their host. On the positive side, their robustness can diminish as they become susceptible to medical interventions or meet the robustness of immune host systems. According to researchers, microbial robustness in terms of the stability of strains is a complex, multifaceted concept that is important for the predictability and efficiency of industrial-level biological production.[37]

In epidemiology, the basic reproduction number or basic reproductive rate, denoted by R_0 of an infection, is the expected number of cases directly generated by one case in a population where all individuals are susceptible to infection. The most important uses of R_0 are for determining if an emerging infectious disease can spread in a human population and deciding what proportion of that population should be immunised through vaccination to eradicate a disease. In commonly used infection models, when $R_0 > 1$ the infection will be able to start spreading in a population, but not if $R_0 < 1$.

The propensity of harmful microbes to multiply in the human body and spread was demonstrated in the COVID-19 pandemic. Estimates for the R_0 for the COVID-19 virus, SAR-CoV-2, vary but values range between 0.4 and 5.7 depending on the data and models used to calculate it. At this R_0, at least 80% of a population would need to be robust enough (through immunity, natural or acquired) to stop the spread or prevent another epidemic.

The COVID experience may well reoccur through the emergence of other zoonotic diseases where a robust and pernicious microbe can defeat the resistance provided by vaccines or antibiotics. With anti-microbial resistance in the human population growing, the prospect of a disease outbreak of global proportions is increasingly possible, if not probable, and may challenge our assumption that a K-strategy is superior. Climate change is increasing this prospect as habitats are threatened and human-animal contacts increase. The robustness of people to overcome new diseases may well be tested to the full.

Because of their relative simplicity and ability to survive and thrive in a range of hostile environments, the tardigrade may well prove to be more resilient than ourselves. It is therefore worth studying further as a vehicle to understand our own robustness as well as our collective health security.

Chapter 2
Resistance and the
Lodgepole Pine

Nature is the master of resistance.
–John Gilbert Holland

While robustness refers to the inherent capacity of a biological species or system for toughness and durability unaffected by a disturbance (a largely passive response), resistance reflects a fight back in order to maintain the *status quo* or equilibrium (a more active response). Both prevent the disturbance from shutting down the system's processes or activities and amount to a defensive and protective posture—the resolute digging in rather than the brazen assault.

Resistance to external forces can be witnessed throughout the natural world when a species or individual organism comes under attack or there is a danger of potential harm. It is an obvious first response to resist and protect and may stimulate an immune reaction to defeat an invading foreign body when and where such immunity exists. In general, resistance refers to the ability of a species, community or population to withstand a shock or stress and assumes that there is no significant reorganisation or successional change involved. This may otherwise lead to a collapse of the system when a tolerance threshold is exceeded.

In contrast, resilience implies that the system is internally reorganising in the face of disruption while retaining essentially the same function, structure, identity and feedback, perhaps through a mosaic of patches that are at different stages of reassembly. It reflects adaptation rather than equilibrium; it is the ability to recover and change after suffering from a disturbance. Resilience is sometimes defined by a series of R's such as resistance, reliability, redundancy, response and recovery. (See *Chapter 3*.) It is essentially restorative but to a new level. In essence, resilience will determine whether a species will be able to tolerate a disturbance or not through recovery to a post-status level.

Resistance can be positive. By being actively persistent, it is possible to survive immense pressures. Animals, plants and people alike have shown incredible powers to repel the worst that the natural and human worlds can present. Trees such as Mangroves can resist severe tropical storms, the keelback snake (*Tropidonophis mairii*) in Australia has developed increased tolerance to the toxin of the invasive cane toad (*Rhinella marina*)[38], while people in Ukraine try to maintain their land even when war with Russia rages around them. One consideration to acknowledge, however, is that what may look like resistance at a coarser scale may actually be very rapid recovery so the terminology depends on the time window of observation. In the case of humans, mental or psychological resistance has allowed some individuals to come through the extremes of isolation, prison camps and even torture.

There is a downside to resistance as well. If persistence becomes a blind pursuit of a cause, there is a danger that it prevents escape and recovery. It, like robustness, becomes an end in itself, and dogged can become dogmatic. Resistance should not turn into stubbornness or inaction by denying the process of change when the situation demands or allows. Such resistance can deny resilience.

It can lead to individual injury or death and may result in species decline. Furthermore, conservation practices during the first decade of the millennium predominantly focused on resisting changes and maintaining historical or current conditions. This focus has proved to be deficient as the ever-increasing impacts of climate change have highlighted the need for transformative action. It is no longer sufficient to resist alone.

If there is a lack of biodiversity in ecosystems, it can be seriously deleterious. Biological systems with species-poor communities are likely to be less resistant (i.e. lower capacity to resist change) as well as resilient (i.e. lower capacity to recover from change) to disturbance than systems with species-rich communities. Therefore, it is important to examine how the animal and plant worlds express resistance, what techniques they use, and where the dangers may lie by ignoring the boundaries through a successional trajectory. We can all learn from the experience.

***

The lodgepole pine (*Pinus contorta*) is one of those species that resists to a considerable degree the ravages of both forest fires and insect infestations to which other trees may more readily succumb. It is worth, therefore, looking more closely at its capabilities as a resilient tree.

The pine, which is also given the names shore pine, twisted pine or contorta pine, is one of the most abundant and long-living tree species in western North America but occurs widely in other regions. Tree plantations have been grown extensively in Norway, Sweden, Ireland and the UK for their timber. In Iceland, it is used for reforestation and afforestation purposes. It is considered an invasive species in New Zealand along with several other western North American pine species.

The common name lodgepole pine comes from the custom of native Americans using tall, straight trees to construct lodges (tepees) in the Rocky Mountain area. Lodgepole pine was also used by European settlers to build log cabins, and logs from the trees are still used in rural areas as posts, fences, planks and firewood. Resin from the pine has historically been used as glue.

The tree attracts the *contorta* label because of the twisted, bent pines found in coastal areas as well as the tree's twisted needles. The thin and narrow crowned tree can grow to 50 m in height and can achieve up to 2 m in diameter at chest height. The crown is rounded and the top of the tree is flattened, except in dense forests where the tree has a slim, conical crown. The bark is thin, scaly and greyish brown but in coastal areas it can be thick and corky, fissured with a checked pattern.

The lodgepole pine has traditionally been resilient to high temperatures in the summer and low temperatures in the winter. The pine's ability to live in many environments—and to live a long time—gives it a genetic boost that could make it more resilient to climate change than other species. While the pine's range stretches over 33° of latitude, the tree maintains high genetic connectivity meaning trees share a lot of genetic similarities. Despite the deserts, mountains and distance between them, pines in the Yukon still have a lot in common with those in southern California, for instance. That means that those good survivor genes are widespread.

While lodgepole pines are genetically similar, they also adapt swiftly to their local environment which creates genetic variability. There are four subspecies, one of which is sometimes considered to have two varieties. This allows them to colonise different habitats. While the lodgepole pine grows best in warm, wet environments, it can also survive in drier places. It is, therefore, common near the ocean shore as well as in dry montane forests and the subalpine but it is rare in lowland rain forests.

A fungus (*Suillus tomentosus*) is known to produce specialised structures called tuberculate ectomycorrhizae with the roots of a variant of the lodgepole pine (*Pinus contorta* var. *latifolia*). These structures have been shown to be the location of concentrations of nitrogen-fixing bacteria which contribute a significant amount of nitrogen to tree growth and allow the pines to colonise nutrient-poor sites.[39] (See *Chapter 6*.)

The reputation of the tree rests largely on its ability to survive forest fires. In fact, the lodgepole pine is a fire-dependent species, requiring wildfires to maintain healthy populations of diverse ages. This ability does not rest in the generally thin bark of the pine which does not protect the trunk from scorching. Rather, it relies on the tree's ability to reseed itself after the fire has passed.

The pine forest can grow back because it has two types of cones: regular cones that open to release seeds in normal conditions, and special serotinous cones that are sealed shut with resin and open only when exposed to the high temperatures of a fire. This diversity of cones provides options for reseeding depending on conditions.

A regular cone from the lodgepole pine. The other type, serotinous cones, are sealed with resin and open only when exposed to the high temperatures of a fire. Credit: Shutterstock

The seeds germinate where the forest floor is clear and plenty of sunlight shines through the newly opened canopy. Each tree also produces many cones, and this redundancy ensures that even though only a relatively small percentage of seeds sprout the forest can still recover. If an area is burned beyond the point where serotinous cones survive, seeds from other forest tracts nearby may also contribute to regeneration.

Replacement fires affecting lodgepole pines may happen every century or so but can be as frequent as every decade if conditions are repeatedly dry and windy. This timeframe allows the species to regenerate and maintain its place in the forest habitat. That is providing climate change does not increase the frequency of fires to the point where new trees cannot mature sufficiently to grow new cones and generate the necessary seeds. The danger is real.

Researchers found a six-fold decline in the number of lodgepole pine seedlings that re-established in the first year following severe fires in the USA in 2016.[40] In some patches of replacement forest, regeneration rates were significantly lower. Dense, young forests were converted into much sparser ones. The researchers also found that the reburned forests lost significant carbon storage capacity.

Nearly two out of three logs on the forest floor were consumed in the 2016 fires. These pieces of dead wood were carbon sinks, storing carbon that the tree took up while alive. When burned, they release carbon into the atmosphere. Once an old forest burns, it takes about 90 years for the forest to recover the carbon lost. With a warming climate and increased frequency of drought, the forests are likely to burn again in short intervals.

Climate change is having another effect on the resilience of the lodgepole pine. The pine is just one of several North American tree species suffering from climate-related changes. In 2010 in Colorado (USA), an estimated 100,000 spruce trees a day were toppled by a massive infestation of the mountain pine beetle (*Dendroctonus ponderosae*), according to a study by Oregon State University and the Department of Forest Resource Management at the University of British Columbia.[41] The 2010 outbreak covered nearly 210,000 acres of spruce forests, nearly double the size of the affected area the previous year. The state also suffered the loss of hundreds of thousands of acres of lodgepole pine and aspen forests.

Mountain pine beetles affect pine trees by laying eggs under the bark. The beetles also introduce a blue-stain fungus (*Grosmannia clavigera*) into the sapwood that prevents the tree from repelling and killing the attacking beetles with a steady flow of tree resin. The fungus additionally blocks water and nutrient transport within the tree. (For an alternative, beneficial view of the role of fungus, see *Chapter 6.*) On the tree's exterior, this results in popcorn-shaped masses of resin (pitch tubes) where the beetles have entered. The joint action of larval feeding and fungal colonisation kills the host tree within a few weeks of a successful attack.

The threat to the lodgepole pine from the destructive mountain pine beetle has risen as decreasing snow cover and milder winters allow more of the insects to survive from season to season. Pine beetles in the lodgepole pine used to be more selective, leaving the younger and healthier trees alone but today their populations and scent (pheromone) levels are becoming so high they can more easily reach epidemic levels and kill almost all adult trees. Fewer frosts, combined with less snow, favour heavier levels of beetle infestation.

Mature and larger trees of the species can resist limited attacks by mountain pine beetles by deploying natural resin in the tree. While resin flow is a physical as opposed to chemical resistance parameter, it is known that resin contains certain toxins (monoterpenes). Resistance to attack is comprised of a three-stage response of wound cleansing, infection containment and wound healing. The first step of this sequence, wound cleansing, involves the flow of constitutive resins at the point of the attack(s). When exuded in high enough concentrations, the resins can trap and kill attacking beetles before they colonise the tree.

Mountain pine beetles attacking certain pine species have been shown to preferentially attack trees with fewer resin ducts and lodgepole pines that successfully resisted attack by the beetle had more resin ducts in recent growth than did trees that were killed by the beetle.[42] Moreover, fertilisation of the ground with low levels of nitrogen resulted in an increase in resin flow while high levels of nitrogen did not significantly increase resin flow in treated trees. This effect supports the nitrogen-fixing symbiotic relationship with the fungus *Suillus tomentosus* and tuberculate ectomycorrhizae with the roots of lodgepole pine mentioned earlier.

Nonetheless, with a significant infestation, the tree can be overwhelmed. Large outbreaks of bark beetles, including the mountain pine beetle, in lodgepole pine, have been recorded in recent years. Both the threat of pine beetles and associated fungi are curbed by wildfires which, paradoxically, may save the lodgepole pine for a while longer.

***

Resistance to the survival strategies of animals and plants is in-built and strong. It is generally in response to adverse or hostile conditions and can involve both physical and

57

behavioural attributes. The hard carapace of a crustacean-like the European lobster (*Homarus gammarus*), for example, provides armour that resists direct attack by predators while hiding in dark crevices and avoids detection by the same hostiles. There are, nonetheless, limits to which such measures can overcome a determined predator.

For trees like the lodgepole pine, resistance to repeated wildfires also has its limits even with special adaptive measures such as the serotinous cones. Beyond these responses, it can only truly resist by extending its range of distribution to other cooler areas if that is biologically and genetically possible.

What the lodgepole pine demonstrates is an ability to fight both fire and infestations at the same time although there are limits or tipping points to each. The tree uses the same natural resin to contend with two different enemies. Furthermore, it shows that a mutual (symbiotic) relationship with another species can increase the pine's resilience by improving its growing potential. These are important characteristics repeated in other species. In oak and beech trees, for example, the larvae of the black-headed cardinal beetle (*Pyrochroa coccinea*) can attack damaging woodboring beetle larvae that live under the bark and weaken the tree.

In human terms, resistance reflects persistence, a fortitude to overcome adversity by active engagement and a determination and courage to push beyond the difficulties. This persistence has two elements. There are the so-called 'hard', physical elements such as the personal armour of old or waterproof clothing of today. This is equivalent to the lobster's exoskeleton. There are also the 'soft', behavioural skills that provide the stamina to continue.

These can be compared to the lobster's habit of living in murky environments at the bottom of the ocean. Like all animals, there will be understandable resistance limits for people; this may relate to strength and endurance or pain barriers inflicted by, for instance, torture. Every person will have his or her own level of resistance.

Interestingly, there is a correlation between the way the human brain has evolved to deal with resistance and other tests. The left hemisphere of the human brain generally performs tasks that deal more with those 'hard' skills that revolve around mechanics and logic, the more actionable attributes. The right hemisphere, on the other hand, generally performs tasks that deal more with those 'soft' skills centred on creativity and the arts. The more behavioural aspects could include elements such as leadership and trust. Thankfully, the two halves are linked for interoperability.

Overcoming adversity often has broader positive effects. People who repeatedly cope with moderately stressful events tend to become psychologically more resistant and better able to cope with future stress. To express it another way, the experience of coping with challenging situations helps to build active resistance and resilience. The phenomenon is well studied in medicine where, for example, Wolff's Law describes how bones or muscles grow stronger due to external load or repeated exercise (hormesis).[43]

Hence, the term 'muscle memory' is sometimes used to refer to this phenomenon. Hormesis is another example of mild 'antifragility' where the tolerance to a poisonous substance improves from a repeated, smaller dose of the poison.

The objective of resistance is to prevent damage or disruption by providing the strength and protection to resist the danger or mitigate its primary impact. This is fine in normal circumstances when the protection is designed and developed to resist the kind of events that have been previously experienced or those that may occur based on historical records. However, this may not be enough to resist future events or attacks that are novel or extreme.

With climate change and its disruptive consequences, normal boundaries are being exceeded ever more frequently and old probabilities are shattered. This is testing resistance. In the future, climatic disruption can be expected to overwhelm the standards provided by normal protection thus resulting in loss or damage and affecting significant survival outcomes, particularly where the resistance strategy is the only component of a resilience strategy.

People also need to find common solutions to deal with a multitude of challenges rather than a plethora of discrete, siloed remedies that are specific for individual, known situations but often not for the one, unknown that emerges. The danger of concurrent challenges with interconnected or cascading consequences increases the impetus to find solutions that are applicable across the board. That impetus must involve greater collaboration and coherence in our responses.

Symbiosis—the art of living together—can be a good mutually supporting approach for people to help resistance. Psychologically, we use the term symbiosis in a similar way to describe a relationship where two people, organisations or communities function as one, and benefit one another. Yet, in biology, symbionts must be of different species so symbiosis is about the living together of unlike organisms.

In the human body, there is one example of a complex ecosystem—'the ultimate social network'—in the trillions of bacteria and other microorganisms that inhabit our skin, mouth and intestines.[44] 'In fact, most of the cells in the human body are not human at all. Bacterial cells in the human body outnumber human cells by around ten to one.' Because of their small size, however, microorganisms make up only about 1–3% of the body's mass (in a 200 lbs adult, that is 2–6 lbs of bacteria) but they play a vital role in human health.[45] This mixed community of microbial cells and the genes they contain, collectively known as the microbiome, do not threaten us but offer vital help with basic physiological processes, from digestion to growth to self-defence.

One microorganism called *Bacteroides fragilis*, which lives in some 70 to 80% of people, helps with human resistance to disease. It keeps our immune system in balance by boosting its anti-inflammatory arm known as T cells. These cells play a major role in recognising and attacking microbial invaders of the body as well as unleashing the characteristic inflammatory response to infection. Soon after the body ramps up its production of T cells, it also starts producing so-called regulatory T cells whose principal function seems to be to counteract the activity of the other, pro-inflammatory T cells. One particular sucrose molecule (Polysaccharide A) that protrudes from the surface of *B. fragilis* is recognised by the immune system and signals it to make more regulatory T cells which, in turn, tell the pro-inflammatory T cells to leave the bacterium alone.[46]

Scientists believe that lifestyle changes over the past century have reduced the level of *B. fragilis* in the body, reducing our resistance and contributing to more autoimmunity and other medical disorders. Scientists have discovered that conditions from Alzheimer's to asthma can be linked to the composition of our microbiome. With this knowledge, they may be able to influence these ailments through genetic engineering of the biome's bacteria. Such an approach is being studied in cows with the aim of reducing the level of methane generated by bacteria in the cow's stomach (rumen).

Another important recent discovery has been a bacterium that can resist and control mosquito-borne diseases in humans. Researchers from the pharmaceutical company GSK have stumbled across a microbe at their research centre in Spain after noticing the mosquitoes they were used for malaria research could reduce the infection of the *Plasmodium* parasite by up to 73%. A bacterial strain (TC1) of *Delftia tsuruhatensis* lives inside the mosquito's guts and is naturally occurring in other environments. It secretes a small molecule known as a neurotoxin (harmane) which appears to inhibit the early stages of the malarial parasite growing in the mosquito's gut. When the research team fed the same strain to other mosquitoes, it seemed to block the parasite from infecting them.[47] The virus-fighting bacterium *Wolbachia pipientis* has also shown particular promise against dengue fever in trials and is already being used in some areas of the world.

From the micro to the macro, resistance can be witnessed at the national and geopolitical levels. Perhaps the most pertinent example in 2023 is the Russo-Ukrainian conflict.

Here, the Ukrainian people have displayed remarkable resistance (and robustness) to an existential threat to their national identity. This resistance comes from their belief in the sovereign integrity of their homeland and their collective spirit of independence. It generates a level of national morale and a strength of character which is likely to continue even if partially defeated on the ground. The ethos is helped by a ruthless enemy who engenders a hatred of Russians that will persist for generations.

Another population that has demonstrated resistance—sadly in the face of the same enemy—is the Finnish one. In the Winter War of 1939–40 as a result of a Soviet invasion, the Finns withstood repeated attacks in bitter conditions before being forced to accept a so-called peace treaty.[48] The experience of losing many people and nearly a tenth of their territory had a profound effect on Finnish psyche and subsequent political positioning. It is generally acknowledged that the main reason Finland prevailed throughout the 105-day war was because of its forces' motivation to resist. Finnish soldiers were fighting for their country, their families and their sovereignty.

Like today's Ukrainians, they also knew the territory they were defending and deployed tactics that were suited to fighting an inflexible foe. However, the Finns were eventually overcome by a stronger foe and had to surrender a proportion of their land to the Russians: the Ukrainians may have to do the same.

The Ukrainian and Finnish experiences reinforce the point that, even at the national level, resistance has an emotional dimension as well as a physical one. Although the animal and plant kingdoms cannot express this duality as we humans can, they nonetheless exhibit some remarkable characteristics which will be tested further as the world becomes more turbulent and uncertain. Those who cannot adapt will face an uncertain future.

Chapter 3
Recovery, Redundancy and the Fire Ant

Nature is flexible and resilient. Nature likes redundancy and dispersion.

–Robert Frenay

If individual animals and the colonies in which they thrive are to survive shocks and stresses, they need to absorb the worst damaging effects and recover as soon as possible. Recovery to a stable, functioning state is the minimum for survival; recovery to the *status quo ante* is the better option; recovery to a higher state that reflects a state of adaptation to the new circumstances is the best option. Recovery means repairing any damage, both internally or externally, after absorbing the shocks or stresses to allow a level of continuity that is functionally and organisationally meaningful.

The ease with which recovery can occur depends to a degree on the extent to which resources and reserves are available to repair the damage. That is usually referred to as redundancy. Standby capabilities present an opportunity to replace damaged assets or functions and allow more time to mount the recovery whether that be measured in spare supplies, alternative production or simply time to think. A network has in-built redundancy through the duplication of assets: if one element is lost, another can take its place.

One issue that arises from redundancy is the question of whether additional assets or functions are wasteful, even inefficient. Why have more bodily capabilities than a single creature needs, particularly if those capabilities may be needed only in emergency or recovery situations? Witness the number of legs of a centipede, the number of termites in a nest or the replications in a DNA sequence in the genetic code. Despite this apparent paradox, and trying to survive often with few or dispersed resources, redundancy is common in the natural world. This is particularly true in the way many animals reproduce. The K-strategy of biological reproduction allows for greater redundancy in the expectation that large numbers of individuals will not survive to adulthood. (See *Chapter 1*.)

Natural duplication can be attributed to a variety of concepts such as safety in numbers, overwhelming potential adversaries, overcoming injury or errors in replication, allowing specialisation, ensuring population sustainability, etc. Rafe Sagarin (2012) offers a review of the benefits and why 'adaptive redundant' strategies have paid off in terms of biological survival despite the energy expended. He writes: 'the combination of redundancy and the inevitable variability and change of nature provides both the drive for evolutionary innovation and the means to carry it out'.[49]

There is another aspect worth considering under the heading of redundancy; that is the value of collaboration between multiple organisms. No animal, plant or person is an island, and we all gain strength and resilience by collaborating with others to achieve species success and sustainability. Nonetheless, collaborating, like redundancy in general, can sometimes come at a cost as it may mean sacrificing individuals or characteristics for the greater good of the species or community.

Social insects that specialise in creating colonies such as ants and bees are good examples of how collaboration can help achieve recovery and build resilience. The sheer number of social insects in colonies allows for a good degree of redundancy in this recovery effort. Redundancy allows for a reserve of assets that means not only can losses be tolerated but also role specialisation can provide a variety of ways to overcome challenges.

Social insects also display a valuable attribute of being able to 'force multiply' both by swarming in large numbers to overcome predators or by clustering when the need arises in nests for joint tasks. These skills are mirrored in people— think of football matches for both swarming and clustering; in effect a form of crowd dynamics. We can therefore learn much from the activities of animals such as the fire ant.

Members of the fire ant (*Solenopsis invicta*) species, which can be found in both South America and subtropical regions of the USA, are social insects that live together in vast underground colonies that can number individuals in the hundreds of thousands. They are aggressive, stinging insects that swarm over other small animals: they can strip carcasses to the bone in a matter of a few hours.

Unlike many other ants which bite and then spray acid on the wounded, fire ants bite only to get a grip and then sting (from the abdomen) and inject a toxic alkaloid venom (solenopsin). This is a painful sting for people, a sensation similar to being burned by fire (hence the name), and the after effects of the sting can be deadly to sensitive people. Fire ants are more aggressive than most native species so have pushed many species away from their local habitat.

Fire ants are renowned for their ability to survive extreme conditions but not the extremes endured by tardigrades. They do not hibernate but can survive cold conditions, although this may be costly to the ant populations as large parts of a colony may die if there are several consecutive days of extremely low temperatures. Furthermore, while other underground insects may drown during severe flooding, Fire ants have well-developed mechanisms that help ensure their survival. The first of these involves being able to float. Floating is possible in part because of the waxy body covering and small, bubble-retaining hairs that help keep the ant waterproof.

The other mechanism is the ability of fire ants to create water-repellent life rafts that can float for days or weeks without drowning the ants. Rafts can consist of many thousands of individuals. The insects crawl over each other and grip the legs of their fellow ants with claws or jaws, forming interweaving patterns like a waterproof fabric. The grip is so strong it would be approximately equivalent to a person dangling six full-grown elephants from the top of a building.

The floating technique allows the ants to relocate to new, potentially drier environments. While drifting, the ants still need oxygen so workers frequently exchange places as they float. Ants in the water on the raft's bottom layer come to the top layer where they can move freely while others take their places below. Those below the water are helped by trapped air pockets that surround their bodies and make the raft buoyant.

The ants trap large air bubbles under the water at depths much greater than the scale of a single ant. All life stages of the fire ant colony, from queens to eggs, form these living rafts. Worker ants carefully protect the queens in the middle and may carry eggs in their mouths.

Scientists have shown that fire ants do not actually seek to clump together in water. Instead, they try to shove each other away. Research has shown that only when ten or more ants are close together in water, a property of surface tension called the 'Cheerios effect' (a form of capillary action) push them together, saving their lives despite their best efforts to avoid contact.[50] Once their legs entangle, it makes a stable hold and creates a fire ant raft. If there are fewer than ten ants, the raft will break up.

In experiments, flowing water created the most pressure at the leading edge of the raft where ants encountered the flow directly. Ants at the trailing end of the raft felt the least amount of pressure. To compensate, the raft continually changed shape so all the ants could stick together and no one ant had to bear the main brunt of the oncoming stream. The researchers found in similar experiments that rafting ants consumed almost 43% more energy than ants on dry land.[51]

The larger the raft, the less energy any individual ant had to generate. Also, the faster the ants in a raft move, the more those rafts would expand outward, often forming long protrusions rather than a circular pancake. The ants may use these extensions to feel around their environments, searching for logs or other bits of potentially dry land.

A floating raft of fire ants. Capillary action pushes the ants together until they find dry land. The raft will only persist if there are more than ten individuals involved. Credit: Shutterstock

It is believed the rafting mechanism occurs spontaneously without the need for any central decision-making by the ants. Single ants are not that clever but collectively they become very intelligent and resilient communities.

Fire ants use 'swarm intelligence' or collective intelligence that allows them to solve complex problems such as finding the closest food source, creating complex tunnel systems within their nests and even cooperating to create rafts to ensure the survival of the colony. Swarming is a collective behaviour that demonstrates cooperation at the colony level which is largely self-organised. It is a form of organised crowd control. The group coordination that emerges is often just a consequence of the way individuals in the colony interact.

These interactions can be remarkably simple, such as one ant merely following the scent (pheromone) trail left by another ant. Yet, put together, the cumulative effect of such behaviours can solve highly complex problems, such as locating the shortest route in a network of possible paths to a food source. Researchers hope these findings could aid the design of robots or drones that work in swarms that follow similar rules to the ants. Rafe Sagarin argues that 'decentralised and distributed organisational systems are much better at adapting and thriving in nature'.

***

Comparing the flood risk for the fire ant with that for human conurbations and crops, we both face increasing dangers from climate change which will require both recovery and redundancy skills. Flood risk is growing at an alarming rate across the world, posing increasingly complex challenges to socio-economic systems, infrastructures and the environment. According to estimates by Marsh McLennan, one in three people globally will be threatened by flooding in a 1.5°C warming scenario, which could happen as early as 2030.[52] This percentage would double if there were to be a

2°C rise. One-third of the world's urban areas and nearly half (45%) of the population will be threatened by flooding in a 3.5°C warming scenario, which could happen by the end of this century.

Despite technological advancements, innovations in risk transfer and the availability of a growing portfolio of risk management tools, the costs of flooding have continued to rise, with only 17% of global economic losses being insured between 2007 and 2021.[53] We clearly need to consider better recovery features following flooding (including preparatory actions before any flooding) and to have redundancy mechanisms in place should it occur. Despite this, 88% of disaster-management funds from humanitarian, development and government sources continue to be allocated to post-event response, according to the insurance industry.

People are naturally reluctant to leave their homes and offices behind and move when floods strike—that is unless homes are washed away. We can mitigate the risk by siting homes away from flood plains and towards higher ground or by imaginative solutions that deflect the rising waters. Even in low-lying areas of Bangladesh, for example, the use of deliberately raised earth mounds in tear-drop shapes that run parallel to rivers have proved better able to divert fast-flowing flood waters.[54]

In other locations, we need to prepare more of our premises at risk with ground floor and basement adaptations (e.g. pumps, water-resistant materials, no electrical apparatus) including placing buildings on stilts and or jacks. This needs to be organised on a community level as it is no good having one building watertight when the surrounding area is under water and access therefore restricted. Yet collective defences constructed around ever higher walls, raisable barriers and larger holding reservoirs will no longer be enough to cope with the anticipated sea-level rise due to climate change, and this will particularly true for 16 megacities (out of a total of 23 megacities worldwide) which have shorelines and have significant populations vulnerable to flooding.

The notion of redundancy or duplication is evident in an ant colony but not immediately obvious why. Having many individuals doing the same task but more than is necessary to maintain the colony on a daily basis seems on the surface to be a wasteful use of resources and effort. Redundancy is also puzzling because redundant groups are particularly susceptible to invasion by defectors.

Yet redundancy is a feature that can be found in a wide range of organisms from microbes to humans. One suggestion for this is that redundancy evolves as a by-product of selection when group members decide whether to cooperate or not while being blind to the strategies of others. Accordingly, possessing information about the strategies of the group members might undermine rather than facilitate cooperation within groups.[55]

In human populations, redundancy has long been a common feature of military planners. Ensuring at least a third of your force is not committed to an operation in the first instance and is therefore able to swing into action to plug gaps or conduct diversions is a sound and long-standing one. In business, however, the striving for lean and cost-effective measures has largely removed redundancy and led to the notion of 'just-in-time' delivery.

The concept of just in time assumes a largely frictionless world of open borders, predictable demand and low transport costs, coupled with good stock control through technology. Food supplies in the UK, for instance, are reported to operate within a window of around a week. Here we see the benefits of efficiency but with tight margins that do not accommodate friction should it interfere.

However, with the turbulent and complex world of today, with ever tighter supply chains, the notion of 'just-in-case' delivery is becoming more in vogue. By holding some stocks in reserve or alternative suppliers in the wings, there is a fallback position in case of serious disruption. There is, of course, a judicious balance to be struck between investing in redundancy and driving efficiency, no matter if one is managing food stocks, racing motor cars or flying aircraft. The fire ant and the centipede also reflect this balance and show—through evolutionary success—to have developed redundancy to a level that is both creditable and efficient.

In human terms, swarming like ants is also a technique used by small, dispersed terrorist cells. Using surprise and simultaneity, they can, for example, overwhelm larger defences and exert an effect much greater than their size would otherwise indicate. The concept of 'swarming' of semi-independent groups that can scale up and down depending on the circumstances does not abolish centralised authority but instead balances it with the right kinds of empowerment and self-sufficiency. The terrorist attacks in Mumbai in 2008 were an illustration of this swarming concept.

The same concept can also apply to established, legitimate forces. In the counter-terrorist world, the growing use of special forces has been the obvious and effective response to swarming against an enemy. Small, highly trained forces operating semi-independently and acting with speed and precision can have an impact beyond their size.

An interesting analogy connecting special forces with the effectiveness of swarming in the fire ant is the potency of the sting. One scientist, Justin Schmidt, has discovered that solitary insects tend to have a much milder sting than those organised in complex groups.[56] It appears that stings allow insects like ants to obtain more food, hence build social structures and therefore defend their nests, the workers, the larvae and other members. The greater the danger, the greater the venom's potency is needed. Special forces would probably agree.

Another analogous feature, and one that recurs in other chapters of this book, is the concept of top-down, bottom-up control. This term describes the notion of being able to combine direction from some higher, central authority with that of an ability to act at lower, decentralised levels. On the surface, this looks like a recipe for disaster as messages originate seemingly from two separate points. Nevertheless, the biological world, including people, seems to manage this apparent confusion with considerable skill.

In the case of an army of fire ants, there is a profound adaptive intelligence at the level of the group that allows it to function as an integral whole. While pheromones play a critical role in the top-down control there may also be more complex arrangements at play which have yet to be discovered. At the single ant level, there is a bottom-up capability to negotiate obstacles and forage for food, with a level of empowerment that allows opportunities for habitats and nourishment to be maximised for the benefit of both individuals and the group. Pheromones again play an important part but there seems little conflict with messages that come from the centre of the nest. Some ants may go rogue and be lost, but against the mass action, there is little to affect the resilience of the group.

People also deploy the top-down, bottom-up concept in organisations with varying degrees of skill and success. We generally manage it not with chemical signals but through a suite of social and moral intuitions that enable us to make decentralised decisions while coordinating at scale. On good days, we can follow rules to solve collective problems while making individual decisions that demonstrate spontaneous wisdom. Effective leaders of organisations can judge what central, mission-oriented messages need to be conveyed while allowing staff the latitude the use their initiative and ingenuity to solve challenges in their own way but still meet the central objectives. This is empowerment and can bring out the best in an organisation while making it resilient at the same time. Should the leader be distracted or absent, others know what is expected and can do their best to make the organisation continue to function and hence be resilient.

Zolli and Healy discovered in their investigations that the most effective leaders were those who had the ability to knit together different constituencies and institutions, brokering relationships and transactions across different levels of the political, economic and social organisation.[57] They were directing from neither the top nor the shop floor. Instead, they represented a form of leadership which the authors refer to as 'translational leaders'. When disruption strikes, the presence or absence of such a leader can have a profound impact on the recovery of an organisation.

As we shall see in other chapters, the combination of top-down and bottom-up is not confined to large groups of ants or people. It is also prevalent in single animals where a central brain provides overall direction but there are other ganglia and neural pathways that allow individual actions by, and senses from, separate limbs. Certain creatures have solved the centralisation versus decentralisation issue in other ways that are worthy of further study. (See *Chapter 5*.)

Finally, but importantly, there is the feature of 'community' in both ant and human populations, as well as other animal groups. The association and bonding in a collective give rise to a whole new level of capability, enterprise and innovation that extends beyond swarming and the benefits of force multiplication. A stable group can achieve organised tasks, endure serious disruption and ensure sustainability well beyond individual and generational lifespans. Community resilience is a treasured asset that comes about through strong relationships and interdependencies within the group for the collective good. In an ant colony, the holistic effort, whether facing a flood or famine, means that successive generations can prosper even though the level of individual understanding is limited.

In human communities, on the other hand, elements like identity and community spirit can help towards collective flourishing. A human community works well when it encourages balance and adjusts its behaviours. In a threatening or dangerous situation, say responding to a storm, people are more likely than not to come together and draw on various talents and skills in order to help victims and unite the community. This ability to adapt and persist is, Donella Meadows suggests, down to three characteristics of 'good systems, namely resilience, self-organisation and hierarchy'.[58]

The idea of collective resilience in the context of 'whole of nation' or 'whole of society' is gaining traction in national and governmental debate. Countries are looking at how best all the various parts of society can be brought together in times of crisis to ensure a prompt and successful recovery. The COVID-19 pandemic has shown the importance of this aspect but other systemic risks can be expected to necessitate a mass engagement of populations. The response should be measured in the hundreds of thousands of people, if not millions, but such a task would require considerable organisation and resourcing.

National resilience will require a national effort, involving the public, private, voluntary, charity, trade union and educational sectors. This is not a case of top-down assuming dominance over bottom-up. Even in a national crisis, local communities, acting as self-organising systems, have an intrinsic ability to respond to shocks successfully; they just need the space, power and relationships to do so. The fire ant colony is a microcosm of such a collective effort.

Chapter 4
Preparation and the Brown Bear

Winter is a season of recovery and preparation.

–Paul Theroux

To prepare and plan for a shock or stress—in other words, to anticipate and pre-empt disaster—is very much a human characteristic requiring cognitive skills that require an ability to horizon scan and provide foresight as well as insight. This activity is a crucial ingredient of resilience. It allows the worst effects to be mitigated and recovery to start sooner. The obverse, namely to react at the time of the perturbation, is likely to lead to a certain measure of chaos and confusion.

Without preparation, we would be reactive and generally found wanting which can lead to loss of life or injury.

Being prepared and having a plan do not inevitably lead to avoidance or an easier recovery. As Mike Tyson, the boxer, once said: 'Everyone has a plan till they get punched in the mouth.' Surprises can always floor. Yet having some measure or mechanism to guide a route forward in times of pending difficulty is sensible and potentially life-saving. It does not require precise knowledge of the challenge ahead or its timing but a general approach can be adapted to meet the eventual circumstance. Lessons learnt from past experiences can greatly help in preparation.

Albeit a well-founded human attribute, animals and plants also exhibit a degree of preparation for the vagaries of the environment in which they live. While not having the conscious features conferred on people, they are able to judge, for instance, seasonal changes in advance and prepare for lean times through winter. This could be considered a response to stress rather than a shock.

Trees begin to prepare themselves as soon as they recognise the early signs of winter. One of the most difficult aspects of winter for plants is that water may be frozen at times and hence cannot be absorbed through the roots. Deciduous plants overcome this lack of water by shedding their leaves each autumn before going into dormancy. They also protect their cells from freezing temperatures by moving water from inside the cells to tiny spaces outside which prevents the cells from freezing.

Conifers, on the other hand, are adapted to prevent water loss with thick, waxy coatings on their needles. Some evergreens have special adaptations such as a valve that automatically seals off individual cells that are frozen. This prevents nearby cells from freezing.

Animals, on the other hand, have three options as winter advances: they can flee to warmer climes through migration, they can adapt with a warmer coat or fleece and stockpile food (a form of redundancy) in external stores or internal fat, or they can hibernate until better times arrive. Relatively few animals enter 'deep' hibernation (e.g. bats, hedgehogs, and some small rodents) while others, like the bear, may go into a state of torpor, slowing down their metabolism to cope with the scarcity of food.

Animals other than mammals and birds also change their behaviour in preparation for winter. Fish, frogs, snakes and turtles adapt to colder weather by becoming dormant. Frogs and turtles hide under rocks, logs or fallen leaves. Some even bury themselves in the mud. Since cold water holds more oxygen than warm water, frogs and turtles can breathe with the oxygen dissolved in the water.

But winter survival for those animals that stay in place is not suddenly arrived at, and there is considerable preparation needed if the long winter months are to be endured. It also heralds some unique changes to the physiology of the animal which have lessons for humans.

***

The brown bear (*Ursus arctos*) is found across Eurasia and North America where it is commonly referred to as the 'grizzly' with a demeanour and reputation to match. It is one of the largest living terrestrial members of the order *Carnivora*, rivalled in size only by its closest relative, the polar bear (*Ursus maritimus*), which is slightly bigger on average.

The brown bear is the most variable in size of the modern bears. The typical size depends upon which population it is from, and most accepted subtypes vary widely in size. The male brown bear is on average at least 30% larger in most subtypes. Individual bears also vary in size seasonally, weighing the least in spring due to lack of foraging during hibernation and the most in late fall after a period of feasting (hyperphagia) in order to put on additional weight ahead of hibernation. In summer through autumn, a brown bear can double its weight from the spring, gaining up to 400 lbs of fat on which it relies to make it through winter when it becomes very lethargic. Although bears are not full hibernators and can be woken easily, both sexes like to den in a protected spot during the winter months.

Hibernation dens may consist of any location that provides cover from the elements and that can accommodate their bodies, such as a cave, crevice, cavernous tree roots or hollow logs. Hibernation seems to be initiated primarily by stresses in the environment such as the arrival of snow and a shortage of food (facultative hibernation) but can take several weeks of slowing activity before the animal enters their winter den.

A bear in its winter den. The animal can slow its breathing and heart rate by about three-quarters for months at a time while maintaining a comparatively high body temperature, unlike other hibernators. Credit: Shutterstock

These cues seem to trigger metabolic suppression. A hibernation induction trigger (HIT), a protein present in the blood, might initiate physiological and metabolic changes that lead to hibernation. Bears can exhibit continuous dormancy for up to seven months without eating, drinking, defaecating or urinating. Awakening from hibernation appears to be due to physiological cues steered by the ambient temperature.

During hibernation, brown bears reduce their body temperature by about 3–5°C from active levels of 37.0–37.5°C and heart rate from about 70–80 beats per minute (bpm) to hibernating levels of around 10–29 bpm (bradycardia).[59] The drop in body temperature is modest when compared with other hibernators where often a decline of 32°C or more can be observed: a hibernating Arctic ground squirrel (*Urocitellus parryii*), for example, can exhibit abdominal temperatures as low as -2.9°C and maintain this for more than three weeks at a time.[60]

The physiological adaptations in the bear's tissues and organs are unique and remarkable. Hibernating bears can recycle their proteins and urine, allowing them to stop urinating for months and avoid muscle atrophy: they can recycle urea by reincorporating it into skeletal muscle and other proteins. They stay hydrated with the metabolic fat that is produced in sufficient quantities to satisfy the water needs of the bear, even in lactating bears. They also do not eat or drink while hibernating but live off their stored fat. Despite long-term inactivity and lack of food intake, hibernating bears are believed to maintain their bone mass and do not suffer from osteoporosis. They also increase the availability of certain essential amino acids in the muscle as well as regulate the transcription of a suite of genes that limit muscle wasting.

The fact that bears do not develop deep-vein thrombosis (DVT) when immobile for long periods, as a human could, is attributable to the reduction of a key protein, HSP47. According to recent studies, it appears that this protein plays a role in the response of blood platelets to collagen thereby helping with the clotting of the blood during injury.[61] As people with spinal injuries have lower levels of HSP47, it would suggest that unlike other anti-clotting agents, animals and people can regulate changes to the protein level without major side effects.

While the metabolic rate drops in all hibernating mammals, bears and small hibernators reduce cardiac output during hibernation from the active state but the decrease is much greater in the latter. During hibernation, bears remain in an alert state and are thus able to increase their heart rate and mobility against the non-responsive hibernating state exhibited by small hibernators (obligate hibernators).

The humble hazel dormouse (*Muscardinus avellanarius*) is an example of an obligate hibernator in which the animal's body temperature drops, its heart rate and breathing slow right down, and it adopts a low metabolic rate in order to save energy rather than to have a rest. In autumn, mature dormice prepare for winter by feeding on hazelnuts and other available nuts and berries and start to put on weight. They store the energy as easily accessible liquid fat just beneath the skin. In fact, by holding a sleeping dormouse in a human palm, it is possible to leave fingerprints on the animal's body. Usually, dormice weigh about 20 gm but the heaviest recorded at the end of summer was one found in Devon (UK) at 44 gm.[62]

It is not known what the trigger is for dormice to go into hibernation. As the animal can spontaneously and annually enter hibernation regardless of ambient temperature and access to food, the traditional idea that it may be a combination of factors including temperature, longer nights and body condition is no longer favoured. It is therefore predictive as the animal enters dormancy before the onset of the adverse conditions.

Research has shown that in adult dormice both winter survival and fecundity were negatively impacted by increased average temperatures and higher rainfall, especially when these patterns of warm, wet weather were interspersed with cold periods. It is not uncommon for hibernators to wake up intermittently but frequent waking depletes the adults' energy reserves by the time they wake in spring, thereby hampering their breeding capacity.

Juveniles were impacted before hibernation and over winter. If juvenile dormice do not build up enough fat reserves before winter, their chance of surviving hibernation is slim. That, combined with waking up early or more frequently and being forced to be active when they should be asleep and when there is less food around, has serious consequences too.[63]

Obligate hibernators are characterised by periodic awakenings during which body temperatures and heart rates are briefly restored to more typical levels.

The cause and purpose of these arousals are still not clear, and there are multiple hypotheses on the topic. One favoured hypothesis is that hibernators build a 'sleep debt' during hibernation and so must occasionally warm up to sleep. Other theories postulate that the animal needs to relieve itself of the harmful metabolites that have built up in its body while sleeping.

***

For the brown bear, preparation for winter begins well in advance. It has limited options to avoid the oncoming ravages of winter so fattens up when food is plentiful, prepares a den in which to rest, and waits out for better conditions. Some people would relish such an option! This preparation by the bear is part of what makes it resilient. It shows a degree of being situationally aware of the changing environment and has an adaptability to cope with the oncoming stresses.

It means the bear perceives the natural elements of its environment, can comprehend their significance (sensemaking), and decides on the appropriate actions to mitigate their deleterious, even life-threatening, effects. Situational awareness is a crucial part of resilience and requires the necessary levels of anticipation and planning. This may be modest in the bear but, nonetheless, demonstrates a level of mental agility that people would interpret in themselves as forethought and insight.

Although hibernation is not an option for people so far, scientists have studied how to induce hibernation in humans. Bear hibernation offers important insights into the workings of large mammals, even humans. A better understanding of the process could potentially change our approach to a wide range of human conditions, including stroke and osteoporosis, as well as Parkinson's and Alzheimer's diseases. The ability to hibernate in humans would be useful for several other reasons such as saving the lives of seriously ill or injured people by temporarily putting them in a state of hibernation until treatment can be given. For long-term space travel, human hibernation is also under scientific consideration.

The possibility has moved one step closer with the discovery by a research team in 2023 that hibernation could be artificially triggered with ultrasonic pulses. [64] The researchers used ultrasound to stimulate that part of the brain in mice that regulates body temperature and metabolism. A non-invasive, wearable ultrasound transducer stimulated neurons in the hypothalamus preoptic area of the brain and was able to drop the mouse's body temperature by 3°C for one hour. Moreover, the mouse's metabolism changed from using both carbohydrates and fat for energy to just fat while the heart rate fell by about 47%.

Mice are naturally able to go into torpor in order to survive potentially fatal cold or starvation. Yet the researchers were also able to induce the same state in a rat which does not have the ability to drop its temperature and metabolic rate to avoid danger. Tests on the rat produced a 1°C drop in core body temperature, resembling natural torpor.

On the more mundane, Earth-bound plane, people do seem to react to the coldest months of the year, by slowing down, preserving energies and often laying down extra fat. Winter can be restorative, and it may be no bad thing, even if a natural desire to hibernate until spring is precluded. Food becomes more of the cooked variety and carbohydrate-rich while sleep tends to be prolonged during short, dark days. This is the closest we get to the dormouse's way of shutting down over winter.

The starting point of resilience in the human context is also preparation, and this involves a degree of anticipation and planning. That preparation in turn begins with being aware of how the circumstances may change. People do it all the time. Taking a journey by road or rail, for instance, means planning the route and alternatives, having money at hand to purchase items on the way, and deciding on a suitable wardrobe in case the weather takes a turn for the worse. These may be obvious and simple precautions but they demand forethought and preparation, as well as the all-important mitigating actions.

It is when humans start to look at challenges longer term—not open to the bear or dormouse—that preparation really comes into play as a positive element. A rigorous approach to preparedness can help to bolster our resilience to longer-term risks and help chart a path forward to a more prosperous world. Although each risk requires concerted, specific and customised efforts, several cross-cutting principles can support preparedness across themes. The annual Global Risks Report (2023) by the World Economic Forum (WEF) identified four principles for preparedness in the new era of concurrent shocks, namely: strengthening risk identification and foresight, recalibrating the present value of 'future' risks, investing in multi-domain risk preparedness, and strengthening preparedness and response cooperation.[65]

Risk identification is a well-trodden and refined methodology to help identify the dynamics of change and the greatest potential dangers. The terms 'horizon scanning' and 'scenario planning' have entered the lexicon of risk managers—they are more elaborate terms for analysing the early warning of events and trends. However, the track record of such foresight is not particularly good. Despite many warning systems and processes in place, we consistently fail to see ahead clearly, especially over the longer term. The number of disasters that have been foretold by warning systems or experienced people but largely ignored, with subsequent large loss of life, also indicates that we fail to heed the indicators and take the necessary actions in advance.

As the WEF report states: 'The underestimation of—and, therefore, lack of preparedness for—emerging macro risks reflects challenges posed by high levels of uncertainty, low levels of information, conflicting data and cognitive biases.'

The report continues: 'Enhanced risk identification and foresight can be a key enabler for strategic decision-making, agenda-setting and resilience measures, helping to prioritise areas that would benefit from data collection and monitoring, risk controls and resources, and redundancies.' Hence, if we are to address the deficit and prepare more effectively, we need to create systems in which barriers to cooperation are removed, decision-making is decentralised, and agility across an organisation is increased to match the pace at which information can be found and analysed. Furthermore, concentrating on consequences (potential impacts) rather than causes (potential risks) would help get around the problems of uncertainty and interconnectedness in the expanding risk landscape.

In terms of future risks, the WEF report states that: 'Complex challenges cannot be solely solved by short-term decision-making—and yet long-term thinking alone is insufficient in the face of currently unfolding crises. To break the cycle, business leaders and policymakers need to embrace complexity and adopt a dual vision that more effectively balances current crisis management with a longer-term lens.' This duality of vision is particularly relevant when including the major challenges of climate-change adaptation, biodiversity loss and ecosystem collapse in annual plans. Risk preparedness, as surveyed by the WEF, is low on these three risk types.

The environmental challenges illustrate the complexity of dealing with large, multi-domain risks. The provision of food, energy, water and clean air are not discrete areas but have cross-sector relationships and interdependencies. Flooding can affect power supplies which can affect telecommunications which can in turn lead to supply-chain disruption, healthcare interruption, and restricted access to banking services. There is the potential for cascading impacts with secondary and tertiary effects across an area much wider than that first flooded, for instance.

To combat these effects, it is necessary to strengthen preparedness and response cooperation by working across sectors and in partnership with other organisations in a holistic plan. The response needs to be as dynamic as the threat, with innovative multi-lateral solutions tackling the diverse range of potential impacts. While governments are best placed to provide the lead here, it is the combination and coordination of parties on the ground that will have the most effect in rectifying a disruptive situation.

Preparedness does not need to cost a lot of money. Clearly, reserve stocks and alternative supplies do not come cheap but preparedness can certainly save time and money. According to a US agency, every dollar ($) spent or invested on preparation has an overall benefit-cost ratio of up to 13:1 depending on the nature of the disaster.[66] Preparation can be as simple as having a plan but training and rehearsing to implement that plan are essential elements if it not just to be a paper plan in a filing draw.

Simulation exercises, stress testing, gaming and table-top exercises can all be valuable steps to assess processes and procedures and ask the valuable 'what if' questions. They need to be carried out regularly as circumstances and people change. A positive outcome of such exercising is the identification of success stories or promising practices which can help to inspire others, and which can be useful benchmarking aids in highlighting good techniques. The idea of discussing possible future failures should not be discarded but encouraged; failure is often a better teacher than success.

It is important not to look too narrowly at any one scenario when undergoing preparation. Preparation for humans involves a good measure of anticipation and forethought, not an aspect that the brown bear is expected to compete. However, the bear and the dormouse do reveal techniques that could be beneficial to people on our road to resilience.

Chapter 5
Agility and the Common Octopus

Octopuses adapt and survive—maybe it's time we do the same.

–Ann Braden

Agility in the context of resilience is the ability to react quickly to changing circumstances. Agility comes down to being fleet of foot (or feet) and opportunistic. It allows adaptation to be developed in a timely and effective manner. It permits rapid decision-making in the face of dangerous or stressful situations.

To be agile requires a certain degree of brain or computing power (mental agility) to calculate the actions necessary to manoeuvre nimbly and speedily. While the lower animals can respond automatically to stimuli such as threats or injury, it is the reserve of those high creatures with more brain capacity and a developed sensory-motor system to respond in a way in which agility becomes more than an automatic, behavioural response. People and the structures that they have created are at the pinnacle of agility.

In advanced animals, it is commonly assumed that agility is correlated to age. The younger of the species may be nimbler in both the physical and mental senses than those with more years to attribute; just look at the speed with which young people deal with modern technology and new challenges. However, experience and expertise, especially in the face of danger, do count as agility has a component that requires a careful evaluation of the challenges in order to avoid nugatory work in finding solutions. That experience is also valuable when animals cooperate and operate in groups or through networks.

There is a group of lower, invertebrate animals that have taken a very different evolutionary path to the human race but where, surprisingly, there are some common features that aid agility. That group is the cephalopods which consist of the ten-armed squid and cuttlefish, the eight-armed octopus, and the multi-tentacled nautilus. The octopus, of which there are around 300 different species, has evolved without a shell (only a beak remains), allowing it to squeeze into crevices that others are denied.

Although humans and octopuses diverged on the evolutionary tree over 200 million years ago, we have both developed a high brain capacity but with very different structures, as well as an eye structure which is remarkably similar and provides good vision. These two common characteristics allow us both to be agile in our discrete worlds and smart. Among the many characteristics we do not share are the social aspect of living and the use of technology to help with agility. If one looks beyond the divergent evolutionary path, the octopus is a fascinating creature that is worthy of its agile status.

**

The common octopus (*Octopus vulgaris*) is usually but not exclusively a solitary creature. Yet it does have a complex nervous system and excellent sight and is among the most intelligent and behaviourally diverse of all invertebrates. Octopuses have large brains and nervous systems for their size. The common octopus has around 500 million neurons in its body: people have around 100 billion! Yet the octopus is in the same range as various small mammals—about as many neurons as a dog—and much larger than other invertebrates.

Unlike the centralised nervous system of most vertebrates, that of the octopus is decentralised with only about one-third residing in the brain. This organ is doughnut-shaped and, strangely, wrapped around the gullet (oesophagus). The remaining two-thirds of the nervous system are spread throughout the body. With mini-brains (ganglia) in every tentacle, of which there are eight, each arm can act independently, giving the animal the ability to taste, touch and move without direction.

Each sucker on an octopus's arm may have 10,000 neurons to handle taste and touch. When the octopus is approached, it may extend an arm to investigate. In fact, the octopus seems to make decisions with its tentacles.

The centralised brain can exert top-down control when necessary. In fact, some kind of mixture of localised (bottom-up) and top-down control seems to be at work. This means the animal can make decisions faster at the point of contact. However, just how a distributed nervous system works, especially when it is trying to do something complicated like moving through water and finding food, is yet to be understood.

As with other bilateral animals, the octopus has some form of memory and a means of learning, enabling past experiences to be brought to bear on the present. The animal shows enhanced learning skills that come with experience and stealth. This ability cannot be inherited as young octopuses learn nothing from their parents with adults providing no parental care beyond tending to their eggs until hatching.

In maze and problem-solving experiments, octopuses have shown evidence that can store both short- and long-term memory. In the laboratory, octopuses can readily be trained to distinguish between different shapes and patterns. They have also been observed in what has been described as play, namely repeatedly releasing bottles or toys into a circular current in their aquariums and then catching them.

The agility of the octopus allows it to take advantage of an unusual situation. This demonstrates the animal's capacity to think ahead and plan accordingly. It was reported that in one marine laboratory, the staff discovered that one octopus was getting out of its tank, going to the other tank, opening it, eating the fish, closing the lid, going back to its own tank and hiding the evidence. That agility extends to the use of tools which is relatively rare in the animal kingdom and is generally a good indicator of the ability to learn. For instance, an octopus has been observed assembling two halves of a discarded coconut shell in order to hide inside.[67] Among invertebrates, only octopuses and a few insects are known to use tools.

Some form of memory introduces the concept of learning, enabling past experiences to be made relevant to the present. Octopuses can learn to unscrew jars to obtain food inside, negotiate simple mazes, move a lever in a tank for the same purpose, and even turn off lights by squirting water at light bulbs to fuse the power supply. This shows a basic level of awareness and adaptation according to the circumstances that prevail. All this goes beyond simple learning by reward and punishment (operant conditioning).

The octopus is a soft-bodied animal. The only remnant of its former vestigial outer shell is a beaked mouth at the centre point of the eight limbs. The soft body can radically alter its shape, allowing octopuses to squeeze through small gaps since there are no bones to worry about. The range of places through which an octopus can squeeze is limited only by the rigid beak.

If the beak fits through, the rest of the octopus will, too. Hence, agility is the octopus's second nature as a contortionist. The siphon is used both for respiration and for locomotion by expelling a jet of water.

Surprisingly, the octopus has blue blood and three hearts. The blood is blue because the protein (haemocyanin) that carries oxygen around the octopus's body contains copper rather than iron as we have in our own haemoglobin. The copper-based protein is more efficient at transporting oxygen molecules in cold and low-oxygen conditions so is ideal for life in the ocean. If the blood (called haemolymph in invertebrates) becomes deoxygenated—when the animal dies, for example—it loses its blue colour and turns clear instead. An octopus's three hearts have slightly different roles. One heart circulates blood around the body, while the other two pump it past the gills, to pick up oxygen from the surrounding water.

Octopuses also have large optic lobes, areas of the brain dedicated to vision, which are important to their lifestyles. Vertebrates and cephalopods separately evolved 'camera' eyes with a lens that focuses an image on a retina. Octopuses appear to be able to recognise individuals outside of their own species, including human faces. They have an ability to adapt to the special circumstances of captivity and to their interactions with human keepers.

Octopuses are sometimes called the chameleons of the sea. Using a combination of pigment, nerves and muscles, the animal manipulates its chromatophores to change its external appearance and match its surroundings. Credit: Shutterstock

This is not a unique behaviour—some mammals and crows can do it too—but it is rather unusual. *Scientific*

American reported a story from the University of Otago in New Zealand where a captive octopus apparently took a dislike to one of the staff. Every time the person passed the tank, the octopus squirted a jet of water at her.[68]

Octopuses use camouflage when hunting and to avoid predators. To do this they use specialised skin cells which change the appearance of the skin by adjusting its colour, opacity or reflectivity. The main colour-producing cells (chromatophores) contain yellow, orange, red, brown or black pigments; most species have three of these colours, while some have two or four. Other colour-changing cells are reflective iridophores and white leucophores. This colour-changing ability is also used to communicate with or warn other octopuses.

Octopuses can create distracting patterns with waves of dark colouration across the body, a display known as the 'passing cloud'. Muscles in the skin change the texture of the mantle to achieve greater camouflage. In some species, the mantle can take on the spiky appearance of algae; in others, skin anatomy is limited to relatively uniform shades of one colour with limited skin texture. Octopuses that are diurnal and live in shallow water have evolved more complex skin than their nocturnal and deep-sea counterparts.

A 'moving rock' trick involves the octopus mimicking a rock and then inching across the open space with a speed matching that of the surrounding water.

Aside from humans, octopuses are preyed upon by fishes, seabirds, sea otters, pinnipeds, cetaceans and other cephalopods. Octopuses typically hide or disguise themselves by camouflage and mimicry; some have conspicuous warning colouration (aposematism) or exhibit deimatic behaviour (startle display). (See also *Chapter 9.*) Deimatic displays involve suddenly creating bold stripes, often reinforced by stretching out the animal's arms, fins or web to make the animal look as large and threatening as possible.

The blue rings of the four types of highly venomous blue-ringed octopus (*Hapalochlaena* genus), for example, are hidden in muscular skin folds that contract when the animal is threatened, exposing the iridescent warning. The octopus, despite its small size, carries enough venom to kill 26 adult people within minutes. Less dangerous, the Atlantic white-spotted octopus (*Callistoctopus macropus*) turns bright brownish red with oval white spots all over in a high-contrast display.

There are at least 15 different species of mimic octopus (*Thaumoctopus mimicus*) which can contort their eight-armed bodies into the shapes of other animals that predators typically want to avoid, such as poisonous flatfish, lionfish, jellyfish or even sea snakes. The fact that all of the species it imitates are venomous adds to the likelihood that this is an evolved and deliberate strategy. This variation is seen appears to vary depending upon the particularities of the predators in the area. Factors such as proximity, appetite and environment may all affect the choice that the mimic makes.

An octopus may spend 40% of its time hidden away in its den. Once it has been seen by a predator, it commonly tries to escape but can also use distraction as a ploy with an ink cloud ejected from its ink sac. The ink is thought to reduce the efficiency of not only the visual organs of predators but also the olfactory organs of predators which employ smell for hunting, such as sharks. Ink clouds of some species might act as decoys (pseudomorphs) that the predator attacks instead.

When under attack, some octopuses can lose their arms (tentacle autotomy) in the same way that skinks and other lizards detach their tails. The severed, moving arm may distract would-be predators. Such severed arms remain sensitive to stimuli and move away from unpleasant sensations. Octopuses can replace any limbs lost.

As already noted, octopuses are generally not social creatures, with very few known exceptions. Unlike the great achievements by the arthropods in social groupings (see *Chapter 3*) where complex behaviours have come about through the coordination of many individuals, octopuses have acquired a non-social form of intelligence with a large neural network. This may be because the cephalopods have never evolved on land and have not needed to develop dense associations. It has developed 'a path of lone idiosyncratic complexity'.[69] A Spanish attempt to farm octopuses for their popular meat in closely packed cages, devoid of stimulation, may therefore prove to be both unsuccessful and cruel.[70]

This notwithstanding, scientists made a surprising discovery in 2017 in Jervis Bay (Australia) where the supposedly solitary gloomy octopus (*Octopus tetricus*) was seen to build underwater cities. Congregations of dens were formed from rock outcrops and discarded piles of shells from the clams and scallops on which the octopuses had feasted. Population sizes were small with only around 15 occupants living in the so-called Octlantis or Octopolis.[71] Then in 2018, researchers discovered around 6,000 specimens, mostly females, of the deep-sea octopus (*Muusoctopus robustus*) which had congregated at a depth of over 3,000 metres on the slopes of a hydrothermal vent off the coast of California. This warm site allowed the quicker development of eggs, at the end of which the females died.[72]

City living has its advantages and drawbacks. Frequent aggression, chases and even den evictions were observed among the octopuses living at Octlantis. The researchers say they are not sure what the benefits of living in a densely populated settlement are for these octopuses but it may just be a case of necessity, with limited den spaces available in the otherwise flat and featureless area. The deep-sea garden clearly has benefits for reproduction.

The typical isolationist habit of the octopus may be a reflection of its intellect. Separate studies on hoofed animals have revealed that those individuals less well integrated into a herd, the loner, are better at problem-solving than those deeply embedded in a social group with fellow members of their species.[73] Studies have shown that more independent and less herd-dependent individuals are more likely to interact with novel stimuli or situations (neophiles) when coming across something new. However, animals that are less well integrated into a herd may need to work harder to find food. Less neophobic individuals and socially less integrated ones were more likely to solve complicated tasks. The octopus is certainly high in the rankings of a capable and agile animal that justifies its reputational placement.

***

The octopus has many sentient attributes which can be related to human behaviour and organisations and hence impart some key lessons. The first of these is the way that the animal and people can adjust behaviours to suit the prevailing environment or threatening situation. Unlike the octopus, we cannot change shape or colour (unless perhaps in a rage!) but we do still adjust our physical posture in response to tense or threatening situations—folded arms, furrowed brow, quickening heart rate, etc. We certainly adjust our behavioural responses to cater for different challenges, some of which may be displacement activity.

People have become as sophisticated in their adaptive behaviours as the complex environment in which they live. Some find it too much of a challenge, hence the rise in mental ill health. The ecosystem of the octopus is also very complex, but through a high level of adaptability, it has been able to survive and thrive. [74]

The dispersed nervous system of the octopus, with just a third of its neurons in the brain and the rest distributed between its eight tentacles, is an illustration of a decentralised neural network. This means that the animal can make decisions faster at the point of contact, according to researchers at the University of Washington.[75]

A decentralised network has also been observed in one of the simplest animals, the box jellyfish (*Tripedalia cystophora*) which has no central brain but a cluster of nerve cells around structures called rhopalia. These act as simple processing centres for visual information gathered by the creature's two-dozen eyes. What has been revealed by researchers in Germany and Denmark is that even without a brain the animal possesses associative learning abilities that allow it to find its way around new environments and adapt accordingly.[76]

Unlike the box jellyfish, the dispersed nervous system acting in concert with a central brain in the octopus allows the animal to bring some overall coordination to the movement of the limbs in order to achieve purposeful direction and actions. When an octopus sees a shrimp at a distance, for example, it compresses itself and creeps up, extends an arm up and over the shrimp, touches it on the far side and either catches it or scares it into its other arms. All this means that there is some level of top-down instruction (from the brain) and bottom-up action (from the limbs) to achieve a harmonious partnership. How this works in the octopus remains a mystery.

As was mentioned in *Chapter 3*, there is an obvious requirement to coordinate effectively top-down and bottom-up activities, and it is the role of leaders and managers to combine the two so that output is maximised. Leaders who can seamlessly work up and down and across organisational hierarchies, connecting groups and translating between constituencies can have a significant impact when disruption occurs in the workplace. It does not inhibit the empowering of people so that they can fulfil other tasks when the leadership is detached or disabled. The octopus also empowers its tentacles.

A top-down structure is generally much less adaptable than one that is flat as the chain of command in the former is tightly controlled with key nodes potentially interrupting the flow of information throughout the organisation. Having distributed nodal pathways on the other hand confers a degree of redundancy so that if one node is removed others can take its place without interfering with functionality. An octopus can still thrive after losing one or two of its tentacles.

The human body is not blessed with too many redundant neural pathways, although rerouting is possible to a limited degree after a severe injury. The internet is perhaps a better example of rapid rerouting after disruption and is stronger for it. A multitude of data centres and cable routers, not to mention a host of satellites and the 'cloud', all help us manage prodigious information flows even when parts are disrupted. Perhaps the octopus has evolved an early form of the internet and is successful because of it.

People have taken agility to new levels but in today's complex and turbulent world then the ability to be flexible and adapt to new circumstances are key assets. Agility or nimbleness allows one to change the body's position quickly and requires the integration of isolated movement skills using a combination of balance, coordination, speed, reflexes, strength and endurance. There is also emotional agility which means being flexible with thoughts and feelings so that one can respond to everyday situations. In organisations, it is about rapid decision-making processes that cut through the usual red tape and managerial layers so that decisions that previously required hard-won consensus or an onerous burden of proof can be accelerated and aligned to the organisation's common purpose.

At all levels, agility connects with learning and the capacity to bring past experiences to the fore in shaping new pathways. While a well-recognised faculty in people, it is perhaps surprising that octopuses also exhibit a very flexible learning capability that goes beyond many other animals, especially invertebrates. Humans and octopuses may be on different evolutionary routes but they both understand the benefits of being agile.

Learning in people is a life-long process. It is a process, even culture, that starts in childhood. Supporting both children and adults in formal and informal educational opportunities facilitates learning and resilience. It also applies to large organisations where collective 'muscle memory' is invaluable in helping to power and steer a successful path for the longer term. Work by management consultants McKinsey and Company asserts that 'Public and private organisations that focus on building resilient leadership and talent can create a virtuous circle of improvement: an adaptable organisational environment will attract needed talent and be better placed for resilience to achieve sustainable growth.'[77]

While people have a recognised tendency to repeat errors despite knowing better, there is human strength in that more often than not we do manage to learn from past failures or omissions to improve the future. Often, more is learnt from failures than successes. Learning can help build an adaptive capacity to respond to novel threats.

Learning lessons comes with experience, awareness, agility and insight. Yet there is a world of difference between identifying lessons (hindsight) and applying them (foresight). All too often, inquiries and post-incident reports are greeted with the refrain that mistakes have been acknowledged and lessons have been learnt. Translating lessons through a learning process into meaningful actions, however, is sometimes hard and painful, and often requires imagination and transformation. Success can confer resilience. This is why it is important to have a system in place that records and transfers positive lessons and effectively contributes to corporate memory.

A part of learning is curiosity and the benefit of play. Playing is the primary way humans and other animals learn how to behave in social settings but if the octopus does not need that interaction then the valid question is why play. The answer may be out of curiosity and stimulation. Curiosity teaches new things and stimulation keeps the neural pathways from deteriorating. If we are denied these attributes, a person can quickly decline and show mental disturbance.

In his insightful book, Rafe Sagarin describes how secrets from the biological world can help us fight terrorist attacks, natural disasters and disease.[78] He believes that the same mechanisms that enable the octopus to escape predators also allow immune systems to ward off new infectious diseases, help soldiers to recognise the threats of improvised explosive devices and aid ways of developing faster ways to detect flu outbreaks.

Military leaders, public health officials and business professionals would all like to be more agile and adaptable, and Sagarin argues that we can do this by observing more animals like the octopus. He writes that reacting to past events and trying to predict future risks will only waste resources. Biological organisms have been living and thriving on a risk-filled planet for billions of years but without planning, predicting or perfecting their responses to complex threats; rather, they simply adapt to solve the challenges they continually face.

Chapter 6
Networking and Mycorrhizae

Nature is pretty good at networks and self-organising systems. By contrast, social systems are top-down and hierarchical, from which we draw the basic assumption that organisations and order can only come from centralism.

–Nicholas Negroponte

Biological communication is often defined by how affected an organism is by the transfer of information between the sender and the receiver. Signals from the sender effect a change in the receiver by imparting information about the sender's environment. Scientists are cautious when determining if the transfer of information benefits both senders and receivers.

Communication is a vital part of resilience beyond any individual. To communicate with more than two individuals means that some form of network or partnership operates between the communicators. That connection may be casual or formal, basic or sophisticated. Generally, the higher up the evolutionary tree, and with ever greater social interaction, the greater the nature and extent of the networking.

Networking with other individuals or species provides a greater perspective of the common challenges as well as alternative solutions needed to overcome them. It gives strength through numbers while reinforcing robustness and resistance. (See *Chapters 1 and 2*.) The ways of communicating and networking can be as varied as the message content. For people who may go beyond the spoken or written word, there are facial expressions, eye contact, body gestures, touches, drawings, etc. Animals use many of these features to a greater or lesser degree. Plants must use a different language.

We have generally thought of plants, and trees in particular, as silent, disconnected individual organisms, competing for water, nutrients and sunlight, with the winners shading the losers and suffocating the weaker. There is now a substantial body of evidence that shows instead that trees of the same species are communal, and can often form alliances with, and communicate between, trees of other species. Trees have evolved to live in cooperative, interdependent relationships, maintained by communication and a collective intelligence similar to an insect colony. It creates for the trees something like a forest internet or, as Peter Wohlleben describes in his book *The Hidden Life of Trees* (2016), a 'social security system'.[79]

One means of communication in plants is via chemicals which can travel from one individual to another through the air or roots and elicit changes. These chemicals warn the plants of, for example, the arrival of herbivorous insects in order that they can coordinate their responses to these pests. The chemicals can be specific to the attacker which infers a sense of taste. The speed of the communication throughout the plant is not particularly fast, perhaps a third of an inch per minute. Hence, it may take several hours for any protective compounds to reach the leaves and ward off the attackers.

Studies have shown that plants can also produce ultrasonic vibrations that other plants and animals may be able to detect. The evening primrose (*Oenothera biennis*) plant, for example, can increase the sugar levels in its nectar in response to vibrations created by pollinating insects. Recent research has demonstrated that plants also make noises when they are stressed through, for example, dehydration or physical damage. Whether other plants are listening is unproven but the fact that noise is happening would suggest that communication is occurring.[80]

So wider communication by an otherwise taciturn biological group is entirely realistic and occurs. A good example of the extent of communication and networking in the plant world can be witnessed in fungal root systems.

***

Trees form mycorrhizae—from the Greek meaning fungus (*mykos*) root (*rhiza*)—which are below the surface connections between the tree roots and fungi. The latter are organisms that lie in evolutionary terms between plants and animals. They have cell walls that are made of chitin, a substance not found in plants but which occurs in bacteria and insects. Fungi cannot photosynthesise and depend on organic connections with other organisms they can feed on. In many but not all instances, the connections are mutually beneficial. Then, the relationship is known as symbiosis which occurs widely throughout the animal and plant kingdoms.

A mycorrhizal network (also known as a common mycorrhizal network or CMN) is an underground network that connects individual trees and plants together and transfers water and essential minerals between participants. The plant or tree communicates its requirement to the network, and the fungus helps direct or filter nutrients to promote growth.[81] The term 'wood wide web' has been used to describe the groundbreaking research of Canadian plant ecologist Suzanne Simard who furnished the definitive evidence for it in the 1990s.[82]

Fungi can cover a vast underground area—multiple acres are possible over decades or centuries in some cases—by developing white fungal threads known as mycelia. The mycelia spread out between tree roots of different trees and take up sugars from the trees and, in return, provide them with vital minerals such as nitrogen and phosphorus. In some ecosystems, plants may be dependent on fungal symbionts for 90% of their phosphorus requirements and 80% of their nitrogen requirements.[83] In other systems, it has been reported that twice the amounts of nitrogen and phosphorus have been found in plants that cooperate with fungal partners than in trees that tap the soil with their roots alone. Mycelia can also greatly increase the tree's root surface so that it can absorb considerably more water than if it operated by itself. Yet, in return, the fungal partners make demands—consuming up to a third of a tree's total food production—thereby allowing it to spread its mycelial tentacles ever further.

The flux of nutrients and water through hyphal networks is thought to be driven by a 'source-sink model' where plants growing under conditions of relatively good resources can transfer carbon or nutrients to plants located in less favourable conditions. A common example is the transfer of carbon from plants with leaves located in high-light conditions in the tree canopy to plants located in the shaded understory where light availability limits photosynthesis.

A rarer example is the plant ghost pipe (*Monotropa uniflora*) which lacks any chlorophyll and hence appears ghostly white. Throughout the summer—usually after rainfall and under beech trees—the plant emerges with each stem bearing a single, nodding flower with several translucent petals. The plant survives by entwining its fine root hairs with the mycelia of underground fungi, allowing it to draw all the nutrients it needs to sustain itself. This technique is called mycoheterotrophy—a relationship whereby a plant obtains food through parasitism rather than photosynthesis.

Mycorrhizal relationships are most commonly mutualistic with both partners benefiting but can be commensal or parasitic, and a single partnership may change between any of the types of symbiosis at different times. (See *Chapter 2*.) There may be hyperlinked 'hub trees' which can be the biggest and oldest trees in the forest with the most fungal connections. With their deep roots, they draw up water and make it available to shallow-rooted seedlings. They help neighbouring trees by sending them nutrients. When the neighbours are struggling, hub trees may detect their distress signals and increase the flow of nutrients accordingly. Plants such as heathers and orchids are unable to photosynthesise and instead rely on carbon transfer from mycorrhizal networks as their main source of energy.

To communicate through the network, trees send chemical substances called infochemicals which act as signals and cues. These substances can be defensive chemicals or nutrients (allelochemicals). Allelochemicals are used by plants to interfere with the growth or development of other plants or organisms. They can also help plants in mycorrhizal networks defend themselves against attack by pathogens or herbivores, and transfer nutrients to affect growth and nutrition.

For allelochemicals to have a detrimental or toxic effect on a target plant, they must exist in high enough concentrations. Yet, much like animal pheromones, allelochemicals are released in very small amounts and rely on the reaction of the target plant to amplify their effects. Due to their lower concentrations and the ease with which they are degraded in the environment, the toxicity of allelochemicals is limited by soil moisture, soil structure as well as microbes present in the earth.

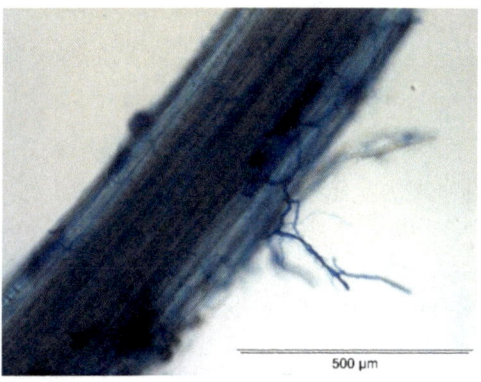

500 µm

The arbuscular mycorrhizal connections with a stem of the rice plant. Rice has emerged as a model to study the AM establishment and functioning, providing insights into potential breeding targets to improve the capacity of the crop.[84] Credit: Shutterstock

A tree may be closely associated with certain types of microbes. For example, the roots of oak and pine trees are surrounded by ectomycorrhizal (EM) fungal networks that can build large underground networks in their search for nutrients. EM fungi are a highly diverse and polyphyletic group consisting of 10,000 fungal species. Their associations tend to be more specific and predominate in temperate and boreal forests. Maple and cedar trees on the other hand prefer arbuscular mycorrhizae (AM) which burrow directly into trees' root cells but form smaller soil webs.

AM networks predominate among land plants and are formed by 150–200 known fungal species, although true fungal diversity may be much higher. It has generally been assumed that this association has low host specificity. Still other trees, mainly in the legume family (related to crop plants such as soybeans and peanuts), associate with bacteria that turn nitrogen from the atmosphere into usable plant food, a process known as 'fixing' nitrogen. (See *Chapter 2*.)

One interesting aspect of the value of mycorrhizal networks concerns seed germination. Studies have shown that the seedlings of the Douglas fir (*Pseudotsuga menziesii*) in the Oregon Mountains (USA) grew better when planted with hardwood trees compared to unamended soils.[85] Douglas firs were found to have higher rates of EM fungal diversity, richness and photosynthetic rates when planted alongside the root systems of mature Douglas firs and the paper birch (*Betula papyrifera*) compared with those seedlings which exhibited no or little growth when isolated from mature trees. The mycorrhizae joining the pair had greater net carbon transfer potential for the seedling.

In another related study, the establishment of the northern red oak (*Quercus rubra*) in a burned yet salvaged forest was facilitated when acorns were planted near the chestnut oak (*Quercus montana*).[86] However, they did not grow when near AM fungi of the red maple (*Acer rubrum*). Seedlings deposited near the chestnut oak had a greater diversity of EM fungi, and a more significant net transfer of nitrogen and phosphorus contents demonstrating that EM fungi formation with the seedling helped with their establishment.

The results seen in the red oak demonstrated with increasing density, mycorrhizal benefits decrease due to an abundance of resources that overwhelmed their system resulting in little growth. Mycorrhizae networks also decline with increasing distance from parents but the rate of survival was unaffected. This indicated that seedling survival has a positive relation with decreasing competition as networks move further out.

***

Transferring the networking of mycorrhizal fungi to those networking concepts of other plants and animals, including people, is not difficult, even if it may seem surprising both on the surface (metaphorically) and above the surface (physically).

Other communication mechanisms in and between plants are becoming more studied. Scientists are beginning to decipher, for example, slow-pulsing electrical signals in certain plants. Edward Farmer at the University of Lausanne in Switzerland has been studying electrical pulses, and he has identified a voltage-based signalling system that appears strikingly similar to an animal's nervous system, although he does not suggest that plants have neurons or brains.[87] Alarm and distress appear to be the main topics of conversation.

Plants that need water or have recently had their stems cut were found to produce up to roughly 35 pulses an hour while well-hydrated and uncut plants were quieter, making about one pulse an hour. The lack of water causes air bubbles to form in the tissue (xylem) that transports water from a plant's roots to its leaves. When those bubbles collapse, they send out small shock waves into the surrounding tissues. They are produced by cavitation where water tension becomes high enough for the air dissolved within the plant's sap to expand.

These noises can travel through the air and be detected up to a metre away. The sounds resemble popping and clicking in the plant's vascular system. As the noise is ultrasonic—

about 20–100 kHz—it means that it is so high-pitched that only a few animals can probably hear the sounds.[88] They are too high-pitched for the human ear.

Plants can also detect sound vibrations caused by predation or other stresses and can communicate this across leaves and branches. Leaves that had been exposed to an insect attack, for instance, have significantly higher levels of defensive chemicals like glucosinolates and anthocyanins, which make them harder for the caterpillars to eat. Many of the chemicals released to cope with insect attacks turned out to be the same as those that are produced to endure cold weather better: both situations seem to activate similar signalling pathways associated with stress.[89]

Trees also communicate through the air using pheromones and other scent signals. The wide-crowned umbrella thorn acacia (*Vachellia tortilis*), for example, is the emblematic tree on the hot, dusty savannas of sub-Saharan Africa. When a giraffe starts chewing the leaves, the tree emits a distress signal in the form of ethylene gas. Upon detecting this gas, neighbouring acacias start pumping tannins into their leaves. [90] In large enough quantities these compounds can sicken or even kill large herbivores.

Where social interactions occur, communication with other species and individuals is crucial in order to create higher organisational, functional and even technological (in humans), networks that benefit all the participants. These interactions, whether direct or indirect, confer resilience on the respective systems as the whole is stronger by acting in concert over and above the constituent parts acting alone. Yet the outcome does not occur automatically and needs constant attention so as to maintain the links and allow them to flourish. Networking can be hard but often provides benefits that go far beyond the original purpose of the network.

Some scientists have even suggested that CMNs can be compared either to 'socialist' or 'capitalist' systems, or to a 'superorganism'.[91] For the 'socialist' behaviour, individuals are able to have equal opportunities, and resources are distributed more evenly providing benefits for all connected plants. For the 'capitalist' network, CMNs would be privately controlled for the profit of certain groups of plants, increasing therefore competition between connected plants. The 'superorganism' would be an entire ecosystem or large human community.

Mycorrhizae networks are just one of many types of social networks in the plant and animal kingdoms. They illustrate the numerous and diverse ways that organisms communicate and interact with fellow and other species. They reflect the value of creating a social order that benefits the group over the individual. The higher the order of the species the greater the sophistication of the biological communication, aided by using some form of language.

The collective nouns of many animal species e.g. shoal (fish), troop (monkeys), murmuration (starlings), pride (lions), herd (elephants) etc. suggest that there is a natural propensity—that we choose to designate—to form organised groups for better protection and resilience. Besides collective survival, the groups may also help the creatures to be more resilient to human interference and disturbance: the decline in the occurrence of murmurations of starlings may suggest otherwise. Network resilience to perturbation is, nonetheless, fundamental to the continuing functionality in systems ranging from synthetic communication networks to evolved social organisations.

The development of social groups encourages a diversity of physical forms, and role specialisation, as well as greater creativity to overcome challenges. In the fire ant, for example (see *Chapter 3*), workers are haphazardly divided into different size classes, namely minima, minor, media, and major workers. The major ants are known for their larger size and more powerful mandibles, typically used in macerating and storing food items, while smaller workers undertake regular tasks such as caring for the eggs/larvae/pupae, cleaning the nest, and foraging for food. The outcome is enhanced resilience of the species.

Insect colonies are frequently cited as examples of successful social networks. The thousands, sometimes millions, of individuals act as one under the control of a queen which determines the roles of the workers. Until 2000, the largest known ant super-colony was on the Ishikari coast of Hokkaidō in Japan. The colony was estimated to contain 306 million worker ants and one million queen ants living in 45,000 nests interconnected by underground passages over an area of 670 acres (2.7 km^2). Since then, an even larger colony has been discovered in southern Europe.[92]

To be able to function as a network, ants can compare areas and solve complex problems by using information gained by each member of the colony to find the best nesting site or to search out food. The information is conveyed via infochemicals (pheromones) and touch. Bee colonies also have sophisticated communication networks. They developed a sophisticated 'waggle' dance to relay to others (workers and drones) the direction and distance of food and, again, pheromones maintain network harmony. In fact, researchers have deployed traditional network analysis to examine animal social systems and to investigate the links between those systems and observed patterns of associations or interactions in human networks.[93]

One network concept that has some commonality is that of 'clustering'. The power of clustering—in effect, the opposite of 'swarming' and decentralisation (see *Chapter 3*)—is seen in the human context as the gravitational pull of professionals to urban locations where similar skills and talent can be shared in an open, networked way but specialisation can be amalgamated to maximum effect, thereby allowing for faster and more innovative solutions. Clustering can be witnessed in the tech hubs in cities where experts congregate to exchange ideas and negotiate directly with capital investors to promote innovations. More broadly, and beyond the constraints of a pandemic, people like to gather and gain value by forming an association with colleagues around which bonds can form.

For people, neural networks are the basis of our motor and mental capacities. Networks are also the lifeblood of communities and organisations. They allow groups to communicate, coalesce and be creative. They create a space for individuals to meet like-minded peers and share knowledge; ideas and innovation are fostered by this kind of peer-to-peer connection. Overall, they can generate huge value, whether that be for an online or offline community.

For businesses, having a network of people connected through common interests and goals to local communities and customers can boost the bottom line. Companies that encourage their people, both customers and employees, to network regularly outperform their competitors. This is one of the reasons why companies are keen to get employees back into offices after COVID-19 where face-to-face contact—those 'water-cooler moments'—can be enhancing and valuable. Local groups can also foster a collective spirit that has an impact far greater than the constituent parts.

With so many benefits, it is a wonder why more businesses and individuals do not conduct more networking. The issue is that networking can be challenging to do consistently and regularly. Fewer than half (48%) of people say that they consistently keep in touch with their networks and one-quarter admit that they do not network at all.[94] The introduction of hybrid working post-COVID has brought new challenges to solidifying in-office networks and has made the task of managers overseeing staff all the more difficult.

It is, therefore, not surprising that so much effort has been made on social networking using readily available technological enablers. Facebook's business model is based around the idea of community online networking and is driven by the belief that sociopolitical upheavals require stronger, more intimate communities, particularly at the local level. Ironically, and perhaps unintentionally, the use of technical platforms like Facebook allows individuals to immerse themselves in what is showing or being inputted on their screens rather than what is directly facing them across the table. Algorithms and advertising will not necessarily strengthen the wider social fabric; they may lead to what has been called 'social polarisation'.

Online communication needs to be supplemented with, or made secondary to, offline communication as physical communities cannot replicate virtual communities in the depth and richness of direct human interactions and experiences. This is not to undermine the value of electronic networks or apps to aid resilience, particularly ones that adapt to new situations.

Despite the sophistication with which people have taken up networking, we have not let go of using infochemicals in our exchanges. On an individual basis, hormones in our endocrinal system help regulate many bodily and emotional functions—our internal, biological network. The use of perfumes and deodorants conveys a myriad of messages to others in our network and can influence our behaviours. If that did not happen then we would not spend billions on buying the products. The mycorrhizal networks of trees appear to have achieved similar effects for much less outlay.

The fact that different species can live together intimately and collaboratively for mutual benefit—the concept of symbiosis—was discussed in *Chapter 2*. Most multi-cellular organisms have symbionts. But now some biologists believe that the microbiome has been superseded by an even more expansive network. The idea is that all animals and plants are parts of a united superorganism whose components evolve in concert with one another. The name given to these communal creatures is holobionts.[95]

It takes a more holistic view of networks and removes the focus on individual organisms. Common mycorrhizal networks emphasise the holobiont nature of fungi and plants which form horizontal associations (rhizosphere) underground through root hairs, fungal threads, spore hyphae and soil bacteria. The whole is clearly bigger than the parts or individuals and in order to understand the overall effect it is necessary to study the associations in, and transmissions across, the network. Such studies can lead to new solutions in, for example, plant breeding for nitrogen fixation, drought tolerance and insect resistance.

The best-studied holobiont of all is *Homo sapiens*. It is now known that microorganisms within play a part in having a good immune system and when the relationships go awry then a range of diseases can occur. Externally, networks within societies, economies and businesses are also critical to wider human growth and development—even fighting off disease: consider the COVID-19 pandemic response as an example of global networking.

Yet the complexities and dependencies within networks when stressed by a disruptive event can easily lead to cascading effects. Hidden interdependencies can emerge that unexpectedly accelerate impacts. Energy disruptions can quickly affect water, fuel, food, transport and communication services, for instance. Supply-chain disruptions can affect production, delivery and prices more quickly. The war in Ukraine has clearly shown how global the effects can be in energy, food and fertiliser markets.

All this demonstrates that a holistic look at connections and associations is important if we are to understand and mitigate the consequences of major disruptions. A whole-of-society concept when looking at resilience is one example of a holistic approach that is taken by some governments in protecting their populations. Understanding networks and connections better in today's environment is a key aspect of resilience.

Chapter 7
Transformation and the
Large Blue Butterfly

We delight in the beauty of the butterfly but rarely admit
the changes it has gone through to achieve that beauty.
–Maya Angelou

As was discussed in the *Introduction*, it has long been
recognised that resilience has its limits or tipping points.
When these limits are exceeded, the ecosystem could rapidly
change to another status. This shift can also be brought about,
or induced, when animals or plants need to change their
habitats in order to perpetuate their life cycle. Such
transformation is usually referred to as metamorphosis. It
signifies a radical change from one form to another.

Resilience involves a transformation in the right set of circumstances. Transformation requires fundamental and wide-scale change which in the context of resilience and sustainability demands radical, systemic shifts in values and beliefs, patterns of social behaviour and organisational regimes. It is not just a case of building back better but also changing the processes so that the rebuilding can be transformational. In biological systems, resilience refers to the ability of ecosystems to respond to disturbance and environmental change with either gradual adaptation or more radical transformation.[96]

Resilience contributes to maintaining the relative stability of living systems over time while transformative resilience describes a living system's capacity to transform itself in response to changing conditions and disruptions. We need both capacities to navigate a path towards a regenerative future. Transformation, sometimes referred to as regenerative resilience, has been described as a process with three distinct phases: first, preparing for change; second, navigating the transition; and third, building resilience of the new trajectory of development.[97]

Humans, organisations or infrastructures in the built environment also use transformation to achieve new goals when there is sufficient momentum to be radical. We do not use the term metamorphosis but there are similarities with the natural world as components become reordered and rebuilt in a revolutionary rather than evolutionary sense; preserving stability no longer meets the requirement. According to one consultancy, business transformation is about new ways of working, new capabilities and new technologies.[98]

Yet it is acknowledged that such 'transformations are not easy to get right'. It is 'difficult, with less than a third of transformations reaching their goals to improve organisational performance and sustain these improvements over time'. If successful, they can 'boost overall performance through increased revenue, lower operating costs, and ensure better customer satisfaction and workforce productivity'. Beyond the consultancy language, there are common goals here for all transformations.

The one animal group that demonstrates this transformation more clearly than any other, and is perhaps the most famous, is the butterfly (*Lepidoptera* order). Butterflies transform from a plump caterpillar into a winged work of art. They are not unique in going through this drastic life change, called complete metamorphosis (holometaboly). Three-quarters of known insects, among them bees, beetles, flies and moths, develop through four stages: egg, larva, pupa and adult.

Other species, such as grasshoppers and dragonflies, develop from nymphs which look like tiny adults, eating and shedding their skins until they reach adulthood. This incredible transformation has a purpose, namely allowing insects at different life stages to avoid competition for food and hence adapt to exploit seasonal shifts and fresh environments.

***

The large blue butterfly (*Phengaris arion*) is a species of butterfly in the family *Lycaenidae*. The species became extinct in Britain in 1979 but has since been successfully reintroduced with conservation. It can be found across mainland Europe, the Caucasus and parts of Kazakhstan. Also known as the gossamer-winged butterfly, it is one of the largest in the family with a wingspan of up to 5 cm.

The butterfly lives for only a few weeks, beginning life as an egg about the size of the head of a pin. Adult female butterflies usually lay their eggs on low-growing grassland plants where certain types of ants are present. Some place the eggs in protected locations—on the undersides of leaves, for example—where wasps and other predators are less likely to find them.

After about three weeks, the egg hatches and the young larva or caterpillar emerges. It feeds avariciously until it reaches the size of an ant grub when it drops to the ground. The larva has glands that are thought to produce secretions that attract but subdue ants. The larva is also capable of producing vibrations and low sounds that are picked up by the common red ants (*Myrmica*) which take the larva back to their nests. These ant-loving (myrmecophilous) associations are more specifically examples of brood parasitic behaviour similar to that of the cuckoo.

Most butterfly larvae consume large quantities of leaves, and they are very specific about which plants they will eat. Most will eat plants from only a single plant type, called the host plant for that caterpillar, such as wild thyme (*Thymus polytrichus*) or wild marjoram (*Origanum vulgare*) for the large blue; the larvae will die rather than feed on others. However, in the case of the large blue, the larvae are not only treated like ordinary ant larvae but are fed first and the most, even when food is scarce.

A young large blue larva is adopted by a Myrmica sabuleti ant.
Credit: Sarah Meredith, Royal Entomological Society.

This is similar to the behaviour of ants towards young *Myrmica* queens. The behaviour is linked to acoustic mimicry by the larvae of the queen which tricks the ant colony workers into giving them preferential treatment. Some larvae of the butterfly can become predators once in the ant nest, feeding on ant pupae while continuing to pose as a *Myrmica* ant.

The larva spends up to nine months feeding and repeatedly outgrows its skin which progressively splits and is shed. Each stage of moulting is called an instar, and some insects moult up to five times before moving on to the next instar. At the end of its growth period, the caterpillar stops eating and finds a good place to moult into the next stage. It spins a small pad of silk and attaches itself to it, hanging upside down, immobile. The larval skin then splits one last time, revealing the pupa (chrysalis). The caterpillars pupate inside the ants' nest and the ants continue to protect the pupa. (See also *Chapter 9*.)

Inside the pupa, the most dramatic part of the metamorphosis takes place. During this stage, which usually takes from two weeks to several months, the pupa releases enzymes which dissolve the tissues completely to create a soup that would ooze out if the pupa were cut open. Certain highly organised groups of cells known as imaginal discs survive this digestive process. The discs use the protein-rich soup in which they sit to fuel the rapid cell division required to form the wings, antennae, legs, eyes and other features of the adult butterfly. In some species, the imaginal discs remain dormant throughout the larva's life; in other species, the discs begin to take the shape of the adult's body parts even before the larva forms a pupa.[99]

What is even more amazing is the fact that the first imaginal discs to become active are unrecognised by the pupa's immune system which tries to destroy them. Yet the discs multiply faster and faster and link up with one other so eventually the caterpillar's immune system fails from the stress of the struggle and the discs win out to go on to build the butterfly's body. The reason for the immune system attacking the incipient butterfly cells is believed to be because of the creation of a new set of genomic instructions to replace the old, unsustainable system. [100] As Augusto Cuginotti expresses it: 'It's the caterpillar's job to resist the butterfly and the butterfly's job to become stronger because of the opposition to its advance.' [101] This echoes the examples of hormesis in *Chapter 2*.

Just before the adults emerge, the wings of the butterfly inside the pupal case detach from it and the pupa becomes silvery. The adult butterfly emerges from the pupa after three to four weeks, still inside the ants' nest. The butterfly must crawl out of the nest before it can expand its wings.

These associations between lycaenids and ants usually benefit both partners. However, even though the ants may benefit from harvesting food rewards offered to them by lycaenid larvae, they do not depend on lycaenids for survival and reproduction. Instead, they forage on a wide range of other food resources. Similarly, most lycaenid larvae feed on specific plants and are not completely dependent upon the ants with which they may be associated.

Metamorphosis is ultimately a successful strategy because juveniles and adults eat different things. Caterpillars eat nutrient-rich leaves to enable all that developmental change, and butterflies just need to sip nectar. For species with such different developmental forms, parents and offspring are not competing for resources, allowing both life stages to develop independently. When insects metamorphose, they can explore and inhabit places that they could not in earlier larval stages.

***

The transformation of insects, as well as some amphibians and marine invertebrates, through metamorphosis, is a process which qualifies as regenerative resilience. Resilience should not simply be a case of building back to a former existence but of building back better to a higher level. It is an opportunity to change and adapt in the face of a new set of circumstances whereby the refreshed entity is better prepared and ready to face new challenges and environments. This is transformation not just continuity even if that were possible. During the transition, the old system may be challenged and may resist but the new system that emerges can be stronger as a result: in the case of the butterfly, something more beautiful arises.

There is also the lesson here that collective action (by cells, creatures or communities) can overcome resistance from below to release hidden potential. Acting together can achieve more than the separate parts alone. This has resonance for other species and populations, including humans. The vision of imaginal cells in the butterfly linking together in a joint effort to transform an unsustainable entity is powerful and applicable to other creatures.

Transformation may not occur in other domains automatically, perhaps no more than with the pupa. It needs a shove such as a seasonal change or external impetus as the effort required is energy-intensive. Being fundamental, it involves all levels of the organism (or even an organisation), from top down to bottom up. Top-down direction establishes the focus throughout and develops the conditions for performance improvement. Bottom-up improvement gets all parts or people at every level to take a fresh approach to improving performance or solving a problem.

In between, there is a cross-functional redesign to link activities and information in new ways to achieve breakthroughs. Certain experts in human organisational transformation believe that taken together these three approaches make up a 'transformation triangle'—a balanced, integrated framework for combining separate initiatives in building back better. [102] When effort is also expended to digitise non-digital products and services or operations—so-called digital transformation—the regeneration moves to a whole new level of sophistication.[103]

For transformation to be successful, it requires a mission-focused approach, one that has a 'north star' as its objective. Because it is so transformative, it is important to have a clear, collegiate objective around which everyone and everything can coalesce. The insect world has this in-built lodestar and can apply it without the managerial jargon that we humans have developed into a fine art form.

As with insects, transformation in business allows new opportunities to be seized in environments that were unavailable before. Fresh markets can be opened up with a revised structure, allowing innovation and creativity to flourish. New wings may allow take-off to new possibilities. Performance can be improved and processes refined in a way that was previously denied. The goal for its implementation is to increase value through innovation, invention, customer experience or efficiency.

There is a danger here, however. If transformation requires so much restructuring and realignment that the original organisation is lost completely then resilience in the strict sense becomes inappropriate as an entirely new organisation may emerge. This situation becomes close to the metamorphosis of the butterfly.

One example of transformation in practice that links the human and natural worlds is the elevated linear park, greenway and rail trail created on a former New York Central Railroad spur on the west side of Manhattan in New York City, the so-called High Line.[104] The abandoned rail spur, transformed from its original purpose and opened in 2009, has been redesigned as a 'living system' drawing from multiple disciplines which include landscape architecture, urban design and ecology. The line has since become a tourist attraction and spurred real-estate development in adjacent neighbourhoods. Ten years after opening, it had eight million visitors per year.

The park is planted to create a natural habit for many native plant species in a busy city.[105] More than 200 species of perennials, grasses, shrubs and trees on part of the old track were chosen for their hardiness, sustainability, and textural and colour variation. Many of the species that originally grew on the High Line's rail bed were also incorporated into the park landscape. Materials were used to ensure sustainability and the conservation of biological diversity, water resources and fragile ecosystems.

Besides human visitors, the planting has attracted insects into the area. The High Line also has a healthy population of sassafras trees (*Sassafras albidum*) which supports spicebush swallowtail butterflies (*Papilio troilus*). This species of butterfly overwinters in cocoons among the leaf litter.

This urban project demonstrates the power of transformation in the human environment and the benefits that such a change can bring to wildlife in the centre of a major conurbation: it signifies metamorphosis in a metropolis. With climate change occurring at an ever-increasing rate then urban transformation will be required at an equivalent speed. It will require a transformation in socio-economic systems and by extension socio-ecological systems. There is no clearer catalyst for urban transformation than a disaster, actual or pending, and the climate emergence provides an opportunity for both.

For example, providing support to farmers of coffee (*Coffea arabica*) in the tropics with conventional agricultural inputs (e.g. pesticides, seeds, farming techniques) in areas that are already facing climate-driven declines in production is likely to be an unsuccessful strategy.[106] Instead, the use of climate-driven transformative strategies such as the support for alternative land uses (e.g. agroforestry or new crops) that would not require the expansion of agricultural land may be more appropriate. Such strategies could help shift coffee production toward a more sustainable alternative pathway.

Climate change will inevitably put pressure on the value chain and may lead to larger fluctuations in coffee supply and higher volatility of coffee prices received by coffee growers, many being smallholders. Therefore, measures need to be developed and implemented to make smallholder production more resilient to climate change. This includes socio-technical systems in agriculture.

Technology has, and will continue to play, a large part in transformative solutions for the betterment of humankind. The introduction of the internet, mobile phones, social media, and artificial intelligence has paved the way for the Fourth Industrial Revolution. On the battlefield, drones have followed on from longbows, machine guns, tanks and aircraft to transform modern warfare. Quantum technologies and robotics will be sure to have equally transformative consequences.

Some of these developments will improve resilience while others will hold it back. A heavy reliance on the internet and information e-platforms, for instance, has introduced dependencies which would become disastrously evident should the internet ever fall over for whatever reason. Even with modern weaponry and its associated technology, the advances have not revolutionised combat in the current Russo-Ukrainian campaign where slow, grinding attritional warfare and hand-to-hand fighting in trenches have become familiar characteristics. While armies adapt and transform in the face of new threats, and the counter-measures that both sides have adopted in Ukraine have dramatically reduced the net effects of new weapons and equipment, that war looks in many ways more like a conflict from the past than one from an imagined high-tech future. In war, new technology matters but adaptations can dramatically dampen its effects.[107]

Rapid technological advance is where we humans diverge from the plant and animal kingdoms which do not have the same benefits. Yet the future of biogenetics and neurosciences have much to learn from other creatures, some even on the lower levels of evolutionary development. This makes it even more important to preserve biodiversity. It also calls for more metamorphosis.

Chapter 8
Adaptation and the
Common Limpet

Nature utilises cycles of adaptation to allow for evolution.
–Lloyd R Shisler

Imagine for a moment that a boat in which you are sailing in open-water springs a serious leak. To keep the vessel from sinking you first need to address the underlying source of the problem. The response means plugging the hole—that is mitigation. But to remove the water already in the boat and to stay dry, you need to start bailing—that is adaptation.

To stay afloat and save the situation, you need to address both issues simultaneously. Adaptation and mitigation are key elements of dealing with change and enacting transformation. Dealing with the enormity of climate change epitomises the duality.

Strictly speaking, adaptation is a process or action whereas resilience is a condition or capacity with an objective. Adaptation is a key, but often neglected, component of resilience. It allows animals and plants to find innovative and imaginative ways of surviving and thriving, making them more competitive and hence successful. It allows evolutionary development in a changing world and through this process permits new environments to be colonised and exploited.

Adaptation is about change in response to changing circumstances. These can be expected, such as seasonal fluctuations, or sudden and dramatic because of, say, an environmental disaster. The ways animals prepare for winter—migrate, hibernate, endure—are examples of adaptation. (See *Chapter 4*.) In human parlance, risk management is based on concepts like avoid, retain, transfer and mitigate. Besides the last of these, the others are instances of adaptation.

A major attribute of adaptation is the recognition that the situation has or is changing—in other words, a sense of awareness—and that a fresh approach is necessary if survival is to be ensured. For animals and plants, this requires an ability to feel and make sense of the environment: attuned senses can warn of the dangers or difficulties ahead. Besides the obvious ones of temperature change, water and food shortages, some organisms can detect minute vibrational waves in advance of, for example, earthquakes and can warn others of the impending calamity.

For people, acknowledging that there is a developing crisis is one of the first factors that can stimulate a response or change. Refusing to accept the situation or denying the crisis (whether internal or external) can prolong the emergency and delay the reaction. This can be seen with the climate emergency where, besides the climate deniers, efforts to stall the required counter-measures because of cost or personal inconvenience will make adaptation and mitigation that much harder.

A second attribute is the capacity and flexibility to be able to adapt. For some creatures, they will be able to move to more suitable locations in response to shocks or stresses. Fish can seek colder waters, birds can migrate over long distances and people can emigrate over equally long distances. All have consequences for others who may have to adapt themselves. Fisherfolk, for instance, may need to seek out new fishing grounds while health services may need to revise practices as workers migrate to better-paid jobs elsewhere.

Other creatures cannot move and adaptation will be difficult. Take the case of coral polyps. Corals and algae live in a mutually beneficial relationship with each other. Healthy corals are home to algae that photosynthesise, giving the coral energy and their coloured hues while the coral provides algae with shelter. Both rely on each other for important nutrient exchanges for survival, another example of symbiosis.

Yet, when the surrounding water heats up too much, the algae cannot function properly and die, leaving the coral bleached and barren. There is some evidence, and hope, to indicate that certain corals may, however, be adapting to higher water temperatures. Whether through species turnover, genetic adaptation or acclimatisation within the coral microalgal communities, it appears that those corals with some heat tolerance may buy time as the oceans warm up.[108]

The limpet is an example of how one animal has adapted over time to the vagaries of living in the intertidal zone. This is a harsh environment that changes significantly twice a day. Warmer temperatures, both under and out of water, also add to the stress of life on the shoreline. So far, adaptation in the limpet's morphology has allowed the creature to survive and be immensely successful in its environment. As sea levels rise and waters warm further, this animal may have to adapt further.

***

The common limpet (*Patella vulgata*) is a species of sea snail (marine gastropod) that occurs in the waters around Western Europe. It occupies the foreshore or intertidal zone on almost every rocky shore of the UK. With two high tides and two low tides occurring daily in coastal areas, the limpet can be subjected to regular and significant changes in its natural environment. The limpet's shell is about 6cm long, 5 cm wide and 3 cm high. The shell houses a strong muscular foot. Common Limpets are believed to be able to live for up to two decades.

All limpet shells are variations on a simple geometric shape—the cone—but there are broad differences in shell size, the shape of the aperture, the height-to-length ratio, and architectural features on the shell's surface. For many years, studies have been carried out on the variations in its morphology in relation to its position on the shore. The cone-shaped shell is an adaptation that enables the gastropod to thrive on rocks from the high-tidal zone to the low-tidal zone.[109]

Limpets living near the lower shore tend to have the flattest and smallest shells but with the greatest width. This can be explained as they are affected by the strongest waves and are, therefore, most at risk of being washed away. A shallow but wide shell provides the largest area for the muscular foot to cling to the rock. In addition, those animals living on the lower shoreline are underwater for the longest time so the seal of a large circumference shell is not essential to prevent desiccation.

Those limpets thriving on the upper shore are taller with a smaller base to their shells. Being further up the beach means they do not encounter strong waves as much so do not need as large an area for the foot to grip the rock. However, they are at a higher risk of damage due to less frequent contact with water, sunlight, water evaporation and the winds. Their tight grip on the rock enables them to trap some water inside their shell and prevents them from drying out.

Apart from desiccation and wave action, there are other factors that influence the growth of the limpets in different places on the shore. Animals living near the lower shore spend more time underwater so they have more time to graze compared to those living higher up. The amount of food eaten is likely to affect the growth patterns and development of the shells. The animals also secrete chemicals that promote the growth of the shell.

Limpets feed on a variety of things depending on their habitat. Varied species of limpets possess structurally different teeth that function as scraping tools. Common limpets scrape off and feed on algal spores and bits of plant matter from the rocks. They do this with a ribbon-like tongue (radula) which with many teeth.[110]

The radula in the common limpet is longer than the shell itself. It contains 1,920 teeth in 160 rows each of 12 teeth. Limpets that feed on rock substrates have unequally sized, sharp teeth. Limpets that feed on marine plants such as seagrass have broad and flat-topped teeth. The teeth are the strongest natural material known. A study published in the *Royal Society Journal* (2015) concluded that 'the tensile strength of limpet teeth can reach values significantly higher than spider's silk, considered to be currently the strongest biological material, and comparable to the strongest commercial carbon fibres'. [111] This considerable tensile strength of limpet teeth is attributed to a high volume of a reinforcing iron-oxide mineral (goethite) deposited as nanofibres.

The muscular foot of the limpet enables a tight grip.
The high profile of this limpet suggests it lives on the upper shoreline. Credit: Shutterstock

As the teeth of the front part of the radula are worn away with use, they are replaced by more posteriorly positioned teeth. The radula grows throughout the life of the animal. Those limpets living high up the shore tend to have longer radulas than those near low water. This may be because the latter have more opportunity to feed and hence wear down their radulas more quickly. It could also be affected by different algal diets according to the intertidal zonation.

A study of the impact of thermal stress, resulting from higher temperatures brought about by climate change, on the morphology of limpet shells has shown that characteristics such as high-spired and heavily ridged shells may reduce the likelihood of high body temperatures.[112] It has been found that limpet cones with greater height-to-length ratios, such as those on the higher shore, tended to lose heat to convection more readily than those with lower-spired shells. Also, heavily ridged shells lost heat to convection more readily than smoother shells particularly when exposed to high-wind velocities. Hence, these morphological adaptations appear to help the limpet cope with climate change.

**

The morphology of the common limpet shows adaptation in action. Adaptation refers to adjustments in biological systems in response to actual or expected environmental stimuli and their effects. It can apply to all biological systems, humans included, so can involve ecological, social or economic impacts.

Climate change is probably the most recognisable form of adaptation. In simple human terms, countries and communities need to develop adaptative solutions and implement actions to respond to current and future climate change impacts. Adaptation can take many forms, depending on the unique context of a community, business, organisation, country or region. There is no one-size-fits-all solution, and answers can range from building flood defences, setting up early warning systems for tsunamis, switching to drought-resistant crops, to designing and building carbon-capture systems. The key issue is whether climate adaptation can be pursued quickly enough to reduce the impact of a warming planet.

An example of climate adaptation for people that connects with the limpet is the design of buildings to cope with increasing temperatures and stormier weather. Round- or domed-shaped houses with a single-storey and strong foundations are important in building wind-resilient properties. Roofs with multiple slopes can stand up well to strong winds, and by installing central shafts wind force and pressure to the roof can be reduced by sucking in air from outside. Roofs that cover balconies or patios can also be designed to break during strong winds to prevent additional structural damage to the essential parts of the house. This is called frangible architecture or a 'planning-for-damage' approach.

A high-pitched roof pitch can decrease the effect of direct solar intensity and associated solar heat gain. This mirrors the limpet's shape on the higher shore.[113] Structural designs of buildings can also help reduce heat inside buildings. Choosing the optimum orientation (including shading) of buildings, with tall rooms and large openings can improve ventilation without the need for air conditioning. Green roofs can be 16–

22% cooler than typical roofs and can reduce city-wide temperatures by 2.7%.[114]

Trombe walls (i.e. heavyweight structures of concrete, stone or other heavy material) that capture solar heat are used extensively in hot regions while green roofs and reflective surfaces can also reduce temperatures in and around buildings. Additionally, shutters, blinds or window films can do much to shield from the sun's heat. Night purging, when windows are kept closed during the day and opened at night, can help flush out warm air.

In the face of major shifts in climate temperature and precipitation, with attendant vulnerabilities, some conventional strategies that help animals, plants and people to cope or adapt incrementally to climate change may become insufficient in the long term. Transformative or regenerative adaptation i.e. fundamental changes in systems that address the root causes of vulnerability may be needed. (See *Chapter 10*.)

There is a limited understanding of what transformative adaptation looks like in ecological systems and when it can be implemented. One interesting case study relates to certain corals and their adaptation to higher water temperatures. Researchers have found that the transformative adaptation of corals is species-specific. The biological age of corals—as with other animals—is closely linked to the length of so-called telomeres at the end of chromosomes in the genes.

Researchers have found that the telomeres in very stress-resistant corals are always the same length indicating that they have a mechanism to preserve the lengths of their telomeres. In a more stress-sensitive coral species, that also has a shorter lifespan, telomere length is aligned to environmental stress such as temperature fluctuations.[115]

There may be a further explanation of longevity here. This concerns the duplication of certain genes. Many important genes are present multiple times in an organism's genome, conferring a degree of redundancy. The presence of gene duplication could also be a possible explanation as to why corals can live for thousands of years despite being exposed, for instance, to extreme ultraviolet radiation in shallow waters.

The impact of environmental stress levels on an organism's resilience through its genome may be a fruitful line of future research. The correlation of telomere lengths in human chromosomes with age may hold implications for human health. It is a long way from bleached coral to wrinkled skin but further analysis could be a valuable contribution to understanding the impact of environmental stresses on us all.

Transformative adaptation for people may also involve restructuring and reconstruction. It may be characterised by being innovative, multi-scale, system-wide and persistent.[116] In cities, for instance, a review of the adaptative plans to heat stress and infrastructural damages showed that they mostly focused on increasing resilience through, say, resistant buildings (as described above) but rarely included actions with transformative potential such as the development of new land-use plans that restricted the use of areas with high risks and mitigation potential.[117]

For people and organisations, adaptation can remove barriers (silos) and bureaucracy so that nimble cross-working becomes the norm. It also encourages empowerment and entrepreneurialism and embraces innovation and technologies that can accelerate processes and decision-making. Yet adaptation can be resisted as it requires change, and this can unsettle some people. Take, for example, the 'Clunk Click Every Trip' campaign for wearing seat belts to improve road safety in the UK.[118]

This campaign began in 1971 but actions did not become law until 1983 and only after extensive promotion and societal debate. The COVID-19 pandemic has also revealed the lengthy efforts to persuade people to wear masks or get vaccinated. Besides the persistent doubters, there is a need for a strong public message to persuade people of the right cause of action. Communicating the appropriate and consistent message is important to change minds and adapt to circumstances.

In general, large organisations with complex bureaucracies like multinationals and governments have little experience of being, or capacity to be, adaptive. They are often like a super-tanker requiring many sea miles to change direction. It is at the other end of the spectrum where individuals, teams and groups, especially first responders to an emergency, tend to show the greatest degree of adaptability to the changing situation. Regrettably, they often lack the resources or power to transfer their adaptive behaviours to larger swathes of society. Both people and groups learn to adapt better when they are organised to be agile. (See *Chapter 5*.)

The biologist Rafe Sagarin argued that we could and should design solutions that continually adapt rather than find one-time fixes to singular problems. He believed that this is a much better approach than that of reacting to past events and trying to predict future risks which 'will only waste resources in an increasingly unpredictable world'. [119] This is what animals do as they do not have the luxury of risk registers and continuity plans. The complexities of the tide pool for the limpet are not totally dissimilar to the human, societal condition; both require a holistic, adaptive framework to address different problems.

Chapter 9
Deterrence and the
Timber Rattlesnake

Even if a snake is not poisonous,
it should pretend to be venomous.

–Chanakya

One of the ways to fight off an opponent or predator who is threatening harm is to discourage them from acting in the first instance. To accomplish such prevention, it is necessary to convey the impression of superior, stronger capabilities, and this usually relies on some form of outward signalling. In general, the bigger and stronger the animal appears, the less likely it is to be challenged. This deterrent effect can also be brought about by visual, auditory, chemical, physical and tactile responses.

Practical mechanisms that have evolved to deter a predator or competitor are multifarious. They include advertising the presence of strong defences so that the potential meal is not worth it and even harmful (aposematism) by mimicking animals which do possess such defences, startling the attacker, signalling to the predator that pursuit is not worthwhile, distracting, using defensive structures such as spines, and living in a group. Deterrence can therefore take many forms, both behavioural and physical.

The European robin (*Erithacus rubecula*) with its vivid red breast, for example, displays and sings to mark its territory with the intention of deterring intruders. It will vigorously defend its space if that deterrence fails. Plants can also deter predators and competitors. In *Chapter 2*, we saw how the lodgepole pine can use resin to resist and deter infestations of bark beetles. Certain plant species appear to hyper-accumulate the element selenium to deter sap-feeding insects.[120]

Some plants encourage the presence of natural enemies of herbivores which in turn protect the plants. This notwithstanding, there is a cost to deterrence or at least a trade-off in desired benefits. In certain plants, an increase in either deterrence or growth must be balanced by a decrease in the other. In animals, the energy expended in developing vibrant colours or spines must be weighed against the degree of protection conferred.

Signalling or messaging is the basis of deterrence. It can involve either real or false factors. As long as the message has the desired effect, its veracity is less important but it must be credible for the opponent to take notice. Deterrence is a form of passive-aggressive behaviour that allows potentially negative outcomes to be conveyed without the necessity of openly expressing them. There may be a disconnect between what an animal that exhibits passive-aggressive behaviour displays and what it does.

What matters is the perception of and by the opponent or competitor. Generally, the intent is to deter without the need for aggression and possible injury to one or both parties. The animal and human worlds are full of instances where deterrence staves off actual combat and allows both sides to retreat intact. This makes for resilient species and communities.

So far, the human species has relied on nuclear deterrence to ward off nuclear catastrophe. Deterrence theory has become an embedded part of military strategy and is even extended to protect allies and partners. The cost of maintaining a credible and powerful nuclear deterrent is enormous, even though it may never (hopefully) be called upon. The cost is exacerbated by the ongoing technological efforts to overcome the potential opponent's own, usually secretive, developments. This doom loop is something that the animal and plant kingdoms have tended to avoid in their respective evolutionary paths.

It is not difficult to find an advanced organism that displays many of the physical or psychological features of deterrence. One animal that fits the bill, and so is described here, is the rattlesnake.

***

There are over 60 rattlesnake species, most of them within the genus *Crotalus*. All of these are native to the Americas, from southern Canada to Argentina. Among the largest rattlesnakes are those living in the eastern half of the USA. The timber rattlesnake (*Crotalus horridus*), also known as the Banded Rattlesnake, typically ranges from 75 to 150 cm in length, although some are recorded at as much as 210 cm in length. The eastern diamondback can grow up to 240 cm in length, weighs as much as 13.5 kg, and is the largest in its species. One of the smallest rattlesnakes is the pygmy of Florida which averages 30–45 cm, about the same length as a domestic cat.

Rattlesnakes are not usually aggressive and most would flee rather than fight. They typically only attack people when startled or provoked. If provoked, a rattlesnake will not immediately bite. Its first response is to perform a threat display. This behaviour includes lifting its body up from the ground, forming an S-shape with its head and neck and thereby making itself appear larger than it normally is. The snake will also hiss at the threat, vibrating its tail to create the distinctive rattling sound for which the reptiles are famous.

The rattlesnake deploys three main techniques to deter its enemies, which are predominantly people and a few predatory mammals, and to enhance its resilience in its natural environment. The first deterrent technique is camouflage: the animal is superbly concealed by its colourful scales. The second is the possession of a rattle on the tip of its tail which generates a warning sound when startled. The third is a venomous bite which can be deadly to small animals and can cause death in humans.

Camouflage, also called cryptic colouration, is a visual defence or tactic that organisms use to mask their location, identity and movement. Remaining disguised from predators can help survival and hence resilience. It also gives the animal an advantage when ambushing its prey. The colouration in rattlesnakes varies according to their habitat. However, most have dark patterns of diamonds or other geometric shapes on a lighter-coloured background.

Disruptive colouration through high-contrast patterns obscures internal features and breaks up an animal's outline. In particular, edge enhancement creates illusory or 'fake' depth edges around the animal's body. Disruptive colouration often occurs in combination with background matching and together these strategies make it difficult for an observer to visually distinguish an animal from its background.[121]

The rattle is made up of a series of loosely linked, interlocking chambers that when shaken vibrate against one another to create the warning signal of a rattlesnake. Only the bottom chamber is firmly attached to the tip of the tail. At birth, a rattlesnake hatchling has only a small button or 'primordial rattle' which is firmly attached to the tip of the tail. The first segment is added when the hatchling sheds its skin for the first time. A new section is added each time the skin is shed until a rattle is formed. The rattle grows as the snake ages but segments are also prone to breaking off and hence the length of a rattle is not necessarily a reliable indicator of the age of a snake.

In a study of the rattling noise made by rattlesnakes of different species, zoologists found that the sounds were always similar: they have rapid onset, starting suddenly, and reaching full volume in a few milliseconds. They consist of a broadband mixture of frequencies (2–20 kHz) with little energy either in the ultrasonic (above 20 kHz) or in the rattlesnakes' hearing range (below 700 kHz). The frequencies do not change much with time—the rattling after 2 minutes has a similar sound spectrum to that at onset.[122]

The pattern implies that the rattling could serve as a general deterrent device which is designed as a deimatic (startle) display. Its similarity to the broadband, harsh sounds used as warning calls by birds and mammals may enhance its effectiveness. Since rattlesnakes can barely hear the sound, it is unlikely to serve as any form of communication with other snakes of the same species. Finally, the sounds are not in themselves loud enough to cause pain and hence keep predators away.

Each segment of the rattle is added when the snake sheds its skin.
Credit: Shutterstock

Rattlesnakes do not always rattle when surprised. Sometimes there is no time to rattle or the snake is young enough that they do not have one. When they try to warn a predator away, their defensive display is generally dramatic and easy to see. Before striking, they often perform a good deal of preliminary posturing and feinting.

The third deterrent device is the bite. The rattlesnake has solenoglyphous teeth which feature two hollow fangs at the front of the jaw. The fangs are attached to a hinge in the mouth so they can rest against the roof of the snake's mouth, folded safely away. This ensures that the snake does not accidentally bite itself.

When a snake bites into its prey, its fangs unfold and come down onto the prey animal. The fangs are connected to venom glands. The timber rattlesnake can use these fangs to inject a high amount of venom quite rapidly. Potentially, this snake is one of North America's most dangerous species due to its long fangs, impressive size and high venom yield. The dangers are to some degree offset by its relatively mild disposition and long torpor (brumation) period during cold weather.

The venom of rattlesnakes contains both neurotoxins and haemotoxins. [123] Neurotoxins attack the victim's nervous system. They send chemical signals to prevent neurons from communicating with each other. Disrupting that communication can cause muscle spasms and paralysis. It can also lead to difficulty breathing or cardiac arrest.

The haemotoxins prevent blood coagulation. They also reduce the number of platelets, making it difficult for the body to heal wounds and in severe cases may cause internal bleeding and haemorrhaging. Haemotoxins also cause necrosis or cell death. This may result in the skin around a rattlesnake bite appearing blackened.

The exact composition and effects of a timber rattlesnake's venom vary depending on the individual snake. Along the northern territorial range of the rattlesnake, for example, a snake with more haemotoxins in its venom is likely. Along the southern edge of its territory, the rattlesnake has a more neurotoxic venom. In between, some snakes have both toxins in equal measure or none of the stated components.

This variety in venom composition is because different rattlesnake populations eat slightly different prey and fend off slightly different predators. If natural selection favours neurotoxins over haemotoxins to slow down prey, those snakes are more likely to survive and breed. This makes neurotoxic venom more prevalent through natural selection.[124]

Venom is basically the rattlesnake's saliva. However, this is saliva that performs multiple, useful tasks for the snake's survival. A rattlesnake cannot hold onto its prey effectively: it only has its mouth to grasp. If it does not kill its prey with one bite, the prey may fight back and hurt the snake. The venom allows the snake to bite and release its prey.

The venom will affect the prey and slow it down. The haemotoxins in the venom will prevent the wound from closing, giving the rattlesnake a trail of blood to follow. The neurotoxins in the venom will cause the prey to weaken and become paralysed, quickly collapsing so that the snake can catch up and devour its meal. The venom also helps to begin digestion before the snake has even swallowed the prey. Digestion is a long process for a timber rattlesnake as it is unable to chew its food but swallows its meal whole.

While the rattlesnake's colouration provides defence through camouflage, other animals are less subtle and use colour signalling (aposematism) to warn potential predators that their defences make a potential meal either unpalatable or poisonous. The visual cues are bright colours and high-contrast patterns such as stripes. The brighter and more conspicuous the colours, the more toxic the animal generally is. This contrasts with the deimatic displays of the octopus which attempts to startle a predator with a threatening appearance, unsupported by any strong defences. (See also *Chapter 5*.)

A reptilian example of both aposematism and mimicry is the venomous eastern coral snake (*Micrurus fulvius*). This has bright red, black and yellow stripes. The pattern of banding and colour is reproduced by the harmless red milk snake (*Lampropeltis triangulum*) which also inhabits the eastern seaboard of the USA. When two aposematic organisms share the same antipredator adaptation and mimic one other to the benefit of both species it means that fewer individuals of either species need to be attacked for predators to learn to avoid both. This form of mimicry is known as Müllerian mimicry after Fritz Müller, a German naturalist. There are wasps that deploy the same deterrent trick.

Although aposematism and mimicry are not generally associated with people, deterrence in the human population has been around for as long as we have interacted. In principle, deterrence could be said to operate in many human activities and relationships, ranging from the private matter of bringing up children to the public measures taken by society to control crime. Of course, the character and style of deterrence differ in each case.

At the higher end of the interaction, and with resilience in mind, deterrence has become a subject of great interest that is studied by many politicians and academics alike. In general, deterrence works more effectively when it is calibrated, proportionate and credible. It is an interactive activity which requires a broadly compatible degree of rationality by all parties. Proportionality and intention introduce the ethical and moral dimensions of deterrence which are absent from the animal world.[125]

In modern strategic deterrence theory, deterrence encompasses two broad approaches: deterrence by the imposition of costs on the opponent (i.e. deterrence by punishment), and deterrence by making it difficult and expensive for the opponent to achieve their aims (i.e. deterrence by denial of benefit). While the animal kingdom relies primarily but not exclusively on the former, people have developed the latter to a higher, more sophisticated level: think of nuclear deterrence and the long-standing philosophy of Mutual Assured Destruction. A key point here is that a country that is and has shown to be, resilient may be able to persuade more easily a potential aggressor or malicious operator that attempts to weaken its resolve or undermine systems are unlikely to succeed.

Even if unused, deterrence still requires a genuine capability to impose punitive costs, the credibility (in the eyes of the opponent) to carry out the threats, and the means to communicate the warnings. Capability, credibility and communication are commonly referred to as the three Cs of deterrence; they are comparable to measures witnessed in the animal world.

There is one key conceptual similarity between resilience and modern deterrence in people, and that is in thinking of deterrence in binary terms i.e. you either deter an attack or you do not. Today, deterrence and resilience are not absolutes but have shades of grey in between. There is the so-called 'hybrid' zone where a range of activities may go on, some unattributed, that are short of open hostilities. Cyber-attacks are an example of such activities.

Furthermore, because the actors and their methods are constantly evolving in often asymmetric ways, it is difficult to deter all malign behaviour completely. In resilience, there is no final status or destination; it is a journey along many paths, so resilience to one particular threat is not necessarily matched by the same level of resilience to another threat.

This means that whether in deterrence or resilience, a range of responses is necessary. It is no good placing all one's eggs in the same basket. Hence a nuclear deterrent, for example, has a mix of sea-, air- and ground-launched weapon systems (a triad). The deterrent measures of the rattlesnake also constitute a triad.

Interestingly, the disruptive colouration patterns, as witnessed in the scales of the rattlesnake, are deployed in military hardware to disguise or deceive an opponent as to the location of assets. Camouflage ranks highly among the arts of war. Blending in with the surroundings increases survival rates and hence resilience on the battlefield. Thanks to modern innovations such as fractal-colouration patterns, which mimic nature by repeating shapes at different scales, the distance from which a naked eye can quickly detect soldiers wearing even the best camouflage has shrunk, apparently by a fifth over the past two decades.[126] Going forward, multi-spectral camouflage will avoid detection over a range of electronic wavelengths and reduce reflections of light, heat and radar.

For both people and animals, the threat of punishment is usually sufficient to prevent a *coup de grace* from being inflicted. The greater the potential for damage, as well as the ability to be resilient to counter-measures, makes for a formidable reputation. Ukraine may not have deterred the Russian invasion of parts of its territory in 2022 but Western backing for Ukraine in the longer term may well serve to deter other aggressors while potentially sowing the seeds for positive political change in Russia. The practical support to Ukraine, coupled with enlargement as a result of Finland and Sweden joining the Alliance, has enhanced the credibility, and hence deterrence, of NATO so far.

Ukraine has also benefitted from an element of 'proximity deterrence' which has parallels with the pupa of the large blue butterfly. (See *Chapter 7*.) The notion here is that it is possible to deter an aggressor by being associated with a larger body that offers protection all around. In the case of the butterfly, it is the myrmecophilous (ant-loving) associations that give the pupa the protection they need. In the case of Ukraine, it is the proximity of certain facilities to the territories of neighbouring NATO members that tends to deter Russian missile attacks.[127]

The more shipping lanes in the Black Sea that are close to NATO shores, the more likely vessels operation will escape Russian strikes for fear of escalation. Deterrence can work by affiliation.

If communities, corporations and countries are to effect deterrence (by denial) as well as be resilient, the onus goes beyond individuals and groups and involves collective, comprehensive activities. A whole-of-society or whole-of-nation approach is desirable but not easily achieved, particularly when there is no real and present danger around which to muster the population. Nevertheless, such an approach is being developed by many nations with varying degrees of seriousness and effect.

It may be helped by looking at potential consequences (impacts) rather than specific causes (risks). It is simply not possible for people or animals to predict the nature of all types of threats. As Rafe Sagarin pointed out (see *Chapter 8*), it is best to be prepared with the general tools to recover and not be overly concerned with the unique tools to fit just one problem.[128]

Chapter 10
Regeneration and the
European Beaver

Creating mechanisms for ending deforestation and
promoting regeneration of the environment [are] the most
effective ways of achieving net-zero emissions.

–Guilherme Leal

Regeneration is the ultimate stage to resilience. It is the culmination or outcome of the combined acts of preparation, recovery and adaptation. It allows either the full return to some form of equilibrium or the transformation to a new state. Both can be described as bouncing forward. In nature, regeneration can range from the replacement or restoration of a lost or amputated body part such as a limb, branch or organ, to a biological system such as an arboreal ecosystem after a fire or climate fluctuation.

Many animals and plants exhibit regenerative capabilities and hence possess a notable level of resilience. For people, one can speak of urban regeneration or societal regeneration, with even ministers for regeneration being appointed to a high government office. There is also the regeneration of the human spirit after testing or traumatic times, or the restoration of youth by rejuvenation to thwart ageing.

Nature-based solutions (NbS) weave natural features or processes into the human-built environment to promote resilience and climate adaptation. They have been shown to offer significant financial and other advantages, often at a lower cost than traditional infrastructures. These practices are increasingly popular in the design of new infrastructure projects. For example, developers in England are required to quantify and mitigate the biodiversity impact of new projects, and Nature England has created a toolkit to help navigate this regulatory requirement.[129]

International projects are increasing in number and scale: a report by the International Coalition for Sustainable Infrastructure spotlights 20 case studies that elevate the agenda for resilience and adaptation across different infrastructure sectors, including social infrastructure such as schools and hospitals.[130]

Rewilding is one example of regeneration under the NbS category. Rewilding can be defined as the large-scale restoration of ecosystems to the point where nature is allowed to take care of itself. It seeks to reinstate natural processes and, where appropriate, missing species, allowing them to shape the landscape and the habitats within.

According to Rewilding Britain, it can encourage 'a balance between people and the rest of nature so that we thrive together. It can provide opportunities for communities to diversify and create nature-based economies; for living systems to provide the ecological functions on which we all depend; and for people to reconnect with wild nature.'[131] Trials at 23 sites in the UK that have introduced rewilding projects have revealed nearly a doubling of full-time-equivalent jobs and a nine-fold increase in volunteering opportunities.[132]

For NbS to become mainstream, the pace of innovation from business will need to be accelerated through effective actions that incentivise investment in regenerative products and services. Frameworks such as the Taskforce on Nature-related Financial Disclosures[133] and Science Based Targets Network[134] provide important guidance for companies to assess impacts and dependencies. Further positive changes in policies, regulation, innovation and market expectations, accompanied by all-important communication, will be critical to achieving progress.

Take the issue of carbon-capture, usage and storage (CCUS) which is receiving much attention from both scientists and governments. Currently, the only cost-effective, mass way to remove carbon dioxide at scale is through the natural environment: trees and plants are great users and repositories of carbon. Promoting this natural process has numerous additional benefits, including flood control and food resilience. According to a report by the World Economic Forum, 'Natural climate solutions could provide up to one-third of the emissions reduction required to achieve the 1.5°C pathway.'[135]

A public-private partnership approach to tackle the issue would be greatly advantageous. Governments could use regulatory frameworks to prevent harm to the environment while companies could begin evaluating environmental risk as part of their investment criteria. 'Natural assets need to be valued: for instance, pricing carbon or water fairly to influence use where voluntary carbon markets can play a key role. Companies should consider nature-based solutions as part of their bottom-line strategies.'[136]

Yet at the bottom end of the chain is an animal or plant. One animal that has come to epitomise rewilding efforts, and hence stimulate regeneration, is the beaver. It has made a remarkable recovery in the UK in recent years. A beaver youngster (kit) was spotted in London in the summer of 2023 for the first time in 400 years; the sighting comes just a year and a half since the species was reintroduced into the capital city.[137]

***

The European beaver (*Castor fiber*) is nature's busy aquatic architect: it is a formidable tree feller, river changer and wetland creator. Through the building of dams, the digging of canals and the creation of dead wood, beavers create and maintain habitats where an abundance and diversity of life can flourish. Dams impound water and lodges serve as shelters, as well as preventing soil eroded from fields from being lost to the sea. Carbon and nutrients are trapped, thereby improving water quality downstream. The flow of water is slowed, so it ameliorates flooding. Dams have been shown to decrease the impacts of floods by up to 60% by reducing water flow.[138]

As beavers are vegan and do not eat fish or other animals, it has been demonstrated that young salmon grow faster and are in better condition in areas where beavers live. A host of other creatures benefit from their presence including insects, amphibians, birds and mammals. Because of their effect on other organisms in the ecosystem, beavers are considered a keystone species[139]

Beavers are the second-largest living rodents after the capybaras (*Hydrochoerus hydrochaerisx`*). They have stout bodies with large heads, long chisel-like incisors, brown or grey fur, hand-like front feet, webbed back feet and flat, scaly tails. The species differs from the North American species (*Castor canadensis*) in the shape of the skull and tail and fur colour. A beaver coat has 12,000–23,000 hairs/cm^2 and functions to keep the animal warm, help it float in water, and protect it against predators. The body is streamlined like other marine mammals and their robust build allows them to pull heavy loads.

The animals are ideally adapted to their environment. They have large skulls and powerful chewing muscles. They have four chisel-shaped incisors that keep growing throughout their lives. The lower incisors have roots that are almost as long as the entire lower jaw. The strong incisors are coated in an iron-rich protective enamel.

Beavers have one premolar and three molars on all four sides of the jaws, adding up to 20 teeth. The molars have meandering ridges for grinding woody material. The eyes, ears and nostrils are arranged so that they can remain above water when the rest of the body submerges. The nostrils and ears have valves that close underwater while nictitating membranes cover the eyes.

To protect the larynx and trachea from water flow, the epiglottis is contained within the nasal cavity instead of the throat. In addition, the back of the tongue can rise and create a waterproof seal. A beaver's lips can close behind the incisors, preventing water from entering their mouths as they cut and bite into things while submerged.

Beavers can hold their breath for roughly 15 minutes on average but it can be for as long as 45 minutes: typically, they remain underwater for no more than 5–6 minutes. Dives usually last less than 30 seconds and are no more than 1m deep. When diving, their heart rate decreases to 60 beats per minute, only half its normal beat, and blood flow is directed more to the brain. A beaver's body also has a high tolerance for carbon dioxide. When surfacing, the animal can replace three-quarters of the air in its lungs in one breath compared to 15% for a person.[140]

Water is the most important part of beaver habitat; they swim and dive in it, and it provides them a refuge from land predators, restricts access to their lodges and allows them to move building objects more easily. Beavers prefer to use slower-moving streams, typically with a gradient or steepness of 1%, though they have been recorded using streams with gradients as high as 15%. Beavers are found in wider streams more than narrower ones. They also prefer areas with no regular flooding and may abandon a location for years after a significant flood.

Beavers typically select flat landscapes with diverse vegetation close to the water. They prefer trees being 60 metres or less from the water but will roam several hundred metres to find more. Roaming beavers will use certain habitats temporarily before finding their ideal home.

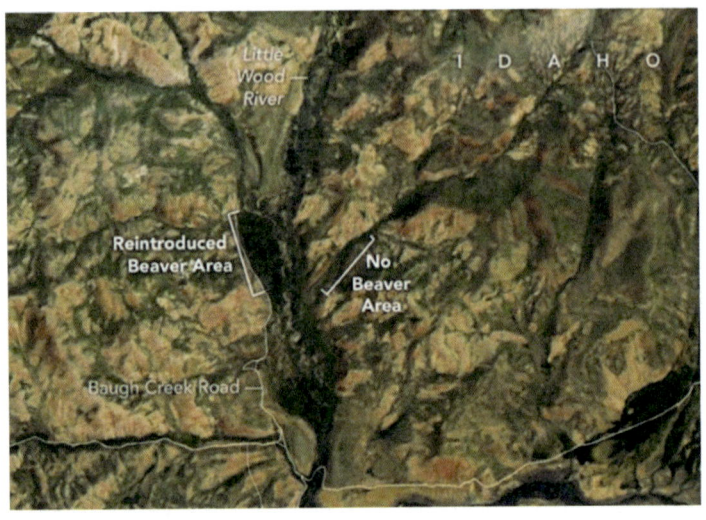

A satellite image of an area in south-central Idaho (USA). The dense green patch indicates more vegetation due to the reintroduction of beavers, while the narrow green patch has limited beaver activity. Credit: NASA Earth Observatory

These include small streams, temporary swamps, ditches and backyards.

Beavers can also offer an NbS to improve the health and function of river catchments. The regeneration or rewilding of landscapes can owe a lot to the activity of beavers. When building their dams, beavers slow or alter the paths of streams and rivers allowing for the creation of extensive wetland habitats. In one study, beavers were associated with large increases in open-water areas.

When beavers returned to an area, 160% more open water was available during droughts than in previous years when they were absent. Beaver dams also lead to higher water tables, both in mineral soil environments and in wetlands such as bogs. In bogs particularly, their dams stabilise the constantly changing water levels, leading to greater carbon storage.

Beaver ponds, and the wetlands that succeed them, remove sediments and pollutants from waterways and can stop the loss of important soils. These ponds can increase the productivity of freshwater ecosystems by accumulating nitrogen in sediments. Beaver activity can also affect the temperature of the water: in northern latitudes, ice thaws earlier in the warmer beaver-dammed waters. Beavers may also contribute to climate change. In Arctic areas, the floods they create can cause permafrost to thaw, releasing methane into the atmosphere.

As wetlands are formed and riparian habitats enlarged, aquatic plants colonise the newly available watery habitat. One study in the USA found that beaver engineering leads to a one-third increase in herbaceous plant diversity along the water edge.[141] Another study found that the width of riparian vegetation on stream banks increased seven-fold as beaver dams watered previously dry terraces adjacent to the stream. Riparian ecosystems in arid areas appear to sustain more plant life when beaver dams are present. (See *Satellite Image*.) Beaver ponds also act as a refuge for water-bank plants during wildfires and provide them with enough moisture to resist such fires.

Beaver activity impacts communities of aquatic invertebrates. Damming typically leads to an increase of slow or motionless water species, like dragonflies, oligochaetes, snails and mussels, to the detriment of rapid water species like black flies, stoneflies and net-spinning caddisflies. Beaver floodings create more dead trees, providing more habitat for terrestrial invertebrates like *Drosophila* flies and bark beetles, which live and breed in dead wood. The presence of beavers can increase wild salmon and trout populations and the average size of these fish.

These species use beaver habitats for spawning, overwintering, feeding and as havens from changes in water flow. The positive effects of beaver dams on fish appear to outweigh the negative effects, such as blocking of migration. Beaver ponds have been shown to be beneficial to frog populations by protecting areas for larvae to mature in warm water. The stable waters of beaver ponds also provide an ideal habitat for freshwater turtles.

Beavers help waterfowl by creating increased areas of water. The widening of the riparian zone associated with beaver dams has been shown to increase the abundance and diversity of birds favouring the water edge, an impact that may be especially important in semi-arid climates. Fish-eating birds use beaver ponds for foraging, and in some areas, certain species appear more frequently where beavers are active than at sites with no beaver activity. In a study of streams and rivers, watercourses with beavers in Wyoming (USA), there were 75 times as many ducks as those without. [142] As trees are drowned by rising beaver impoundments, they become ideal habitats for woodpeckers which carve cavities that may be later used by other bird species.

Other semi-aquatic mammals, such as water voles, muskrats, minks and otters will shelter in beaver lodges. Beaver modifications to streams in Poland create habitats favourable to bat species that hunt at the water surface and use moderate vegetation litter. Large herbivores such as some deer species benefit from beaver activity as they can access vegetation from fallen trees and ponds.

The introduction of beavers in an effort at regeneration is not all positive. Farmers and landowners are sometimes in opposition. Some specific habitats and species of high conservation importance can be adversely affected by beaver populations if appropriate management is not undertaken. Beavers are also likely to have a detrimental impact on certain woodland habitats such aspen (*Populus tremula*) woodland. A lack of woodland regeneration, especially when there is high deer abundance could lead to habitat degradation. On balance, however, the benefits of beaver activity seem to outweigh the deficits.

***

NbS reinforce resilience and help advance sustainability. It is no longer sufficient to bounce back from change but important to build back better for the long term. This involves working with nature and helping to make the natural world better prepared to face climate change and other systemic challenges. NbS, such as rewilding, are designed to protect, sustainably manage and restore natural ecosystems while simultaneously providing human well-being and security benefits. They typify adaptation and resilience projects around the world.

Rewilding, as exemplified by the reintroduction of beavers, is about letting nature take care of itself, enabling natural processes to shape land and sea, repair damaged ecosystems and restore degraded landscapes. Through rewilding, wildlife's natural rhythms create more biodiverse habitats. Natural infrastructures can help replenish groundwater supplies by absorbing and filtering water, in addition to alleviating the ravages of coastal erosion and sea-level rise. They can also help with dealing with the challenges of extreme heat as well as sequester carbon thereby mitigating climate change.

Other NbS projects exist that use existing or rebuilt natural landscapes to increase resilience to climate impacts, such as inland flooding: they can also result in environmental, economic and social co-benefits. These can help absorb precipitation and reduce runoff—one acre of wetlands can store and filter up to 330,000 gallons of water.[143] Another solution is the protection or restoration of riparian buffers, namely vegetated or forested banks to reduce the amount of water entering waterways. Natural systems can absorb up to 90% of the precipitation they receive.

Then there are NbS projects that combine with existing human infrastructure to create hybrid systems that improve resilience to climate impacts. Generally, green infrastructure is a built or engineered solution such as green roofs or bioswales (i.e. long, deep channels of plants and grasses along roads and parking areas that absorb runoff and release water slowly) as well as the use of urban tree canopies. Trees collect raindrops before they hit the ground, giving rain more time to evaporate instead of becoming runoff. Deciduous trees can collect up to 700 gallons/year and evergreens up to 4,000 gallons/year.

NbS can boost local economies where alternatives are scarce. This can help with revitalising both rural and urban communities. When thinking about community resilience in a natural setting, regenerative or active resilience (as opposed to passive resilience or recovery) is a popular term. To some, this may border on tautology as resilience embodies recovery with reconstruction which automatically makes it active. Ignoring the fine distinction, a regeneration-for-resilience (R4R) approach provides a decision-making structure to prioritise limited resources and utilise artificial and natural regeneration management. [144] This makes for the greatest likelihood of success in locations and landscapes.

The aim is to support multi-generational, self-sustaining host populations through restorative techniques that blend human social needs with nature's requirements. It draws on ecological models and systems theory. It depends on a holistic, community-wide approach that builds on resilience to allow a green and sustainable future. This goes beyond the crisis management of discrete disruptive events to long-term, self-organising partnerships across a broad swathe of local and regional groups working with NbS. In the face of overlapping, complex and systemic risks—from climate change to economic insecurity or rising inequality—communities can seed and lead the economic and social transformations necessary.

Communities, both for many animals and people, are often the bedrock of wide-scale resilience. They provide the collective support between individuals to face quotidian challenges and strengthen the ties during more turbulent events. The bonds established provide the motive and energy to survive and thrive. Whether *Solenopsis invicta* or *Homo sapiens*, the need is to restore the external situation to some form of normality and then to regenerate the environment or ecosystem so that it allows the community to continue to flourish.

When discussing regeneration in human communities, the term 'social capital' comes to the fore. The term 'capital' is adopted to reflect the key aspects of complex relationships in societies, enabling societies to function effectively, to be resilient, and to be sustainable. It applies to civic engagement and bonding of all types when mitigating any kind of shock or stress and recovering from the worst effects. Communities are one of the most effective elements of disaster and emergency relief, and all resilience planning should be directed to building up social capital and community infrastructure that can be flexibly deployed at times of crisis.

The attraction of using a capital-based approach is the ability to assess the potential resilience within a society and its environment. For example, the elements of social capital (e.g. trust, networks), human capital (e.g. education, skills) and environmental capital (e.g. biodiversity, carbon sequestration) can be used as indicators of overall resilience. Using qualitative and quantitative data from Japan where an earthquake and a tsunami struck on 11 March 2011, Daniel Aldrich has shown how communities with deeper reservoirs of social capital have higher survival rates and faster recovery times.[145] Given that social capital, like other forms of capital, can be strengthened and created, it can also measurably increase levels of trust and efficacy.

The notion of a whole-of-society or whole-of-nation approach is the next tier that requires R4R. These 'whole-of' terms adopt a broader scope and interpretation of community, one that looks across a country or common location but in the context of the environment. Regeneration here involves a multitude of participants from the government, through farmers and fishermen to businesses and services, and down to individual households. As the challenges to the nation become more complex, as well as turbulent and uncertain, the transformative responses need to be more universal and systemic. Climate change epitomises the risks and the challenges. The reintroduction of the beaver epitomises one successful natural solution.

Chapter 11
Whither Resilience and Humankind?

It is our collective and individual responsibility to preserve and tend to the world in which we all live.

–Dalai Lama

According to the World Wildlife Fund (WWF), the UK is one of the most nature-depleted countries in the world and, despite nature struggling against all odds to survive, more than one in seven native species face extinction and more than 40% are in decline.[146] The WWF's 2024 Living Planet Report believes that 'there has been an average 73% decline in wildlife populations worldwide since 1970'. The report warns that as the Earth is approaching dangerous tipping points it poses grave threats to humanity.[147]

Centuries of farming, building and industry—and more recently and increasingly climate change—have reduced wildlife to a point not seen elsewhere. When compared to other G7 countries, the UK is at the very bottom of the league in terms of how much biodiversity still survives—it has only half of its natural biodiversity left. When compared to all countries in the European Union, only Ireland and Malta come out worse, and the UK is in the bottom 10% of all countries globally.

While the UK has made some gains, the opportunities for nature to bounce back and demonstrate resilience are diminishing. Yet biodiversity matters as we depend on the natural world for the water we drink, the air we breathe, the food we eat, and many medicines that can heal us. This issue is not confined to any one country but affects all countries to varying degrees. One-fifth of the world's countries are at risk of their ecosystems collapsing because of the destruction of wildlife and their habitats, according to an analysis by the insurance firm Swiss Re. [148] With more than half of the global GDP depending on high-functioning biodiversity, the risk of tipping points being exceeded is growing.

While previous human societies have collapsed as a result of the destruction of their environmental underpinnings, the collapse has never before reached the point that the entire human population disappears on a continental scale i.e. mass extinction. The planet has seen five mass extinctions in its planetary history. The danger is that in the coming decades if we continue to damage our environment beyond restorable limits, our current standard of living and even our very existence may be threatened. Short of that, we have already seen the collapse of animal populations like cod on the Grand Banks of North America because of overfishing, while we are witnessing the shift of the Amazon rainforest to a savannah-type mixture of trees and grass within half a century because of deforestation, and the Caribbean coral reefs could collapse within less than a score years. There is a direct correlation, for instance, between a loss in diversity of coral reefs by more than 60% by human activity such as sewage and/or industrial pollution.[149]

For our own survival, we must protect the biome as much as possible. As the preceding chapters reveal, we can learn a great deal from plants and animals on how they survive and thrive, within certain limits. Biological organisms have over millennia been able to respond to significant change to their ecosystems without planning, predicting or tying their responses to complex threats. They simply adapt to solve the challenges they continually face. But our success and theirs cannot be guaranteed if we do not take the necessary actions to help protect their ecosystems and blindly assume there are no tipping points.

We also need to look at our own societal resilience and ask where this is heading. The series of national lockdowns during the COVID-19 pandemic showed, contrary to expectations, that human society at large can adapt to a significant degree when facing challenging times. We can follow national guidelines when we see them in our best interest and life-sustaining. Societal resilience held firm in the pandemic—we were all in this together was a common mantra. On the surface, the pandemic was a great leveller as we were all equally likely to be infected although as time has revealed some ethnic and vulnerable groups were disproportionately affected by the virus.

COVID-19 was a war without the physical damage but a war nonetheless on people, communities and society as a whole. While the precise cause of that particular zoonotic disease has not yet been definitively established, it can be linked to the mismanagement of wet markets trading in animals and, therefore, associated with our inability to treat the natural environment with the respect it deserves. Other zoonotic diseases are sure to follow: the spread of the virus H5N1 in and beyond bird populations is but one example.

Much has emerged since the pandemic on how we should respond to repeat civil contingencies. The UK government has published a framework on national resilience and introduced several functional changes to help make the government and its agencies better prepared. The 'whole-of-society' approach has been a theme of recent high-level reviews but the precise applicability of this approach has yet to be elucidated. Hence, the practical difference such measures will make in our national resilience in a future crisis is awaited. Significantly, one of the elements largely missing from the whole-of-society approach to date has been the integration of the biome in the consideration of a healthy societal outlook.

Beyond the contingency planning and preparation, there is another important question to consider. That is about the residual level of societal resilience that there is across the UK. How ready are we to face and factor in significant disruption to our daily lives and livelihoods? If the example of COVID-19 is anything to go by, perhaps we should be confident.

However, on a wider, non-threat-specific front, the answer is not so positive and the future is less assured.

What is the glue that binds society and allows us to be resilient as a collective, and in tune with nature? Is the level of resilience in the population as a whole declining? The answer to these questions should be found in a set of common values and principles that the majority is willing to adhere to in the face of external challenges. Without them, disorder, even anarchy, could materialise. However, in this modern, multicultural era, these values and principles are increasingly loose and ill-defined. There is an absence of a pole star around which to coalesce when troubles strike. The decline of the religious component in everyday life, whatever one's beliefs, has diminished the number of places to shelter physically and recover emotionally.

The trend has been exacerbated by the increasing isolation and introspection (self-interest) that modern living encourages. We are more inclined to see our world from within the four walls of our properties, and shaped by the technology that clutters our lives and the social media that bombards our spaces, never mind the natural world with which we are intrinsically linked. The daily carriage by car or train to work means that interactions with others are limited and fleeting. In general, we are less inclined to engage with local community groups, other than for sports or hobbies. Volunteering is thankfully alive but a relatively small proportion of people participate in relation to the size of the overall population.

It is perhaps not surprising that there is a general feeling of concern about the direction of travel, disquiet over the plethora of major issues that dominate the news headlines, as well as mental ill health, even unhappiness, at the frenetic speed of modern living. According to a World Gallup Poll (2023) of 147,000 adults in 142 countries, there is a globalisation of gloom with one in three feeling discontented in a negative experience index.[150] This is up from one in four over a decade, with middle and younger age groups particularly affected.

Then there is the inequality gap. According to Oxfam, the five richest families in the UK are wealthier than the bottom fifth of the entire population. While this was less of a factor in the pandemic, it may well rear its head in another disruptive event when those with the means can remove themselves or buy a level of protection that others cannot purchase. Such a situation will contradict the notion that we are all in this together and inhibit popular actions that could be for the general good. The UK has a widening inequality gap—the Gini coefficient worsened by 1.3% in FY2022—that detracts from collective, mutually supporting measures and exacerbates the fragmentation of societal norms.[151]

Taken together, these trends reflect the negatives that detract from a resilient society and a resilient natural environment. They could be dismissed as transient and a phase in our societal development. Yet, and to whatever degree, they discourage the development of resilience for the medium and long term. Resilience needs to be sustainable and systemic. It needs to be present through the highs and lows as shocks and stresses can occur at any time, often on the most inconvenient occasion or sometimes concurrent with other challenges.

If we are to be serious about being resilient, both for ourselves and the biological world around us, it requires a mobilisation of the nation—all communities—that is more than short-term but one that can sustain a long-term regenerative process. It needs a firm narrative and positive strategy that allows for the combination of nature and communities, together with the physical infrastructure, in a balanced and sustainable way.

People are at the heart of designing services and systems that can weather a crisis, and civic engagement is central to capacity-building, but the natural world is the underpinning element that we are often not cognisant of and, therefore, fail to incorporate in our strategies and plans. To act positively requires foresight and imagination, with a view to cultivating the capacity to cope with many plausible futures.

If the depletion in biodiversity, the COVID-19 pandemic, the energy crisis and the climate emergency have shown anything, it is that resilience requires the participation and mobilisation of all or at least a large part majority of the citizens in any country. This means millions rather than a few thousands of ardent enthusiasts. Businesses of all sizes, volunteers, charities, public services, places of worship, trade unions, NGOs, reservists, schools and colleges—all need to be involved in the restoration of the nation and biome, not just after a shock (e.g. a national catastrophe) but also for the stresses in between (e.g. climate change).

The response needs to be coordinated, collaborative and comprehensive. Some countries are already better prepared in this regard than others but there should be no place for complacency. We need to explore and adopt regenerative systems in our food chains, our energy systems, our transport systems, our health and social care systems, our digital systems, and in our natural world.

This means adopting active measures—*a priori*—to communicate, train, organise, command, control and lead disparate communities to a common objective, namely recovery and regeneration. Local communities need to be empowered to act, not just be consumers, and social networks and partnerships need to be strengthened and sustained. When any national infrastructure cannot cope, human infrastructure must be tapped into and called to fill gaps that emergency services are simply unable to address. It is about self-organisation and self-motivation.

There are many good projects underway to help save parts of our rapidly disappearing natural world. Saving endangered birds or marine species, for example, should move beyond the few protected reserves and willing volunteers to be a larger integrated approach to making the country truly resilient—for the whole of society. Supporting more trees and wilderness on marginal land would not damage food security but it could bring fewer floods, less carbon release and more diversity of income to rural areas—all promoting national resilience for the longer term.

Human adaptability can mimic natural adaptation. The same mechanisms that enable a fire ant to survive flooding or the common octopus to escape predators can be used to help us tackle existential threats to our planet. But they will not happen automatically. We need to be proactive with holistic and systemic plans to design resilient strategies for the long term and in combination with others.

These plans need both 'hard' and 'soft' skills—the mechanical or hard skills such as policies and procedures to provide direction and rules as well as the more personable or soft attributes of trust, learning and experience to cope with vital inter-relationships. At the higher level, we need national figures and politicians who can step up to the plate and lead the nation in a direction which recognises the place that the natural world has in our overall resilience. A resilience framework that places emphasis on civil contingencies and fails to acknowledge the decay of the planet as a whole will not be enough to be called a whole-of-resilience approach.

Epilogue

The world's population has in general made significant strides over the last few centuries and particularly over the last half century. The proportion of those earning less than a dollar a day has diminished—albeit still running at around one billion—while those especially in the developed world are better fed, have better health care, and have more wealth. We should therefore remain optimistic.

This notwithstanding, the number of migrants has increased, those civilians killed or injured in conflicts have grown, the wealth divide in many countries has widened, and we are all having to deal with the ravages of climate change. The solution to the growing feeling of insecurity from these challenges lies in how citizens and countries cope with the inevitable change. While people do have a great propensity for finding solutions to challenging problems, it does at times feel as if the Anthropocene era may be all too brief.

If we cannot resolve the increasing range of volatile, uncertain, complex and ambiguous (designated by the acronym VUCA) problems facing the human race, we can at least be resilient to their effects for as long as possible. The natural world provides some of the solutions or indicators to the problems if we can bother to look, learn and listen. If the rate of extinction continues at the current pace, the opportunities to learn from the biological world will continue to diminish, and may never be replaced.

The selection of ten plants and animals in this book is meant to show that we can learn from creatures who are very different to ourselves. The lessons may not be directly applicable but they embody the same principles of resilience that we adopt. The biological world has developed resilience to a finite art—hence, the ability of many species to survive and thrive over millennia. We would be unwise to ignore this and should do our utmost to learn how resilience is applied in as many species as possible. They may hold the secrets to our survival.

Take the African elephant (*Loxodonta* genus) as an example. Sadly, over 30,000 African elephants are killed every year, with the population currently estimated to be around 400,000, a decline of over 100,000 in the past decade, largely because of poaching. This magnificent creature, like other large animals such as the whale, has been found to be less prone to cancer than people contrary to expectation: 5% and 25%, respectively.

The more cells in a body that can divide uncontrollably and spread to surrounding tissue would suggest that a large animal would succumb more often to a disease like cancer. In fact, the lack of correlation between body size and cancer risk gives rise to Peto's Paradox, after the British statistician Sir Richard Peto. An animal like the elephant with 1,000 times more cells than a person not exhibiting an increased cancer risk indicates that natural mechanisms can suppress cancer 1,000 times more effectively than is done in human cells.[152]

The secret appears to lie in a particular gene (TP53) in the elephant which is called the 'guardian of the genome' and seems to repair damaged DNA and dispose of cells it cannot repair. While people have one copy of the gene, each elephant possesses 20.[153] This may have happened via an evolutionary process when the gene arose to protect other processes in the animal. So here is a case of a creature that could help us with understanding our fight against cancer—provided we help it survive and thrive.

It is appropriate to end this book therefore with the elephant. In mythical, religious and literary domains, the elephant is often seen as having human attributes such as strength, intelligence and, supposedly, a good memory.

Some authors have ascribed the adjective 'black' as the idiom for 'not mentioning the elephant in the room', namely an idea visible to everyone but which no one wants to deal with.[154] Another author has spoken of 'black' jellyfish to similarly challenge what we think we know and understand about a subject but which turns out to be more complex and uncertain, sometimes with a nasty sting in the tail.[155]

Perhaps the most widely known idiom is the 'black' swan to refer to those challenges that we had previously unobserved, namely high-impact, highly-improbable events. The term 'Black Swan' was used in the book of that name.[156] It derives from a Latin expression and was coined as such an animal was presumed not to exist: that is until it was discovered in Australia in 1697.

These illustrative comparisons between the animal and human worlds are valuable as they connect us in ways that reveal our fragility in an uncertain world.

To use another idiom—'the canary in the mine'—the natural world highlights our own frailties as well as indicates the dangers ahead if we do not take heed of the warning signs early enough and take evasive actions to avoid a potential collapse of the planet's ecosystem. Animals and plants can undoubtedly offer indicators as well as solutions to many of our challenges.

As the opening quotation by Albert Schweitzer to this book suggested, we also need to look at what is around us in the natural world to see the blooms and benefits. Our constant efforts at growth, largely to satisfy swelling populations and expectations but reducing our natural environment at the same time, are unsustainable for a planet with finite resources. A moral tale for this Anthropocene age can be found in a highly recommended book by Miriam Körner that is credited in the *Acknowledgements*, and echoed in Rachel Carson's prophetic words in 1962: 'I wonder if we have not too long been looking through the wrong end of the telescope.' 'We have looked first at man with his vanities and greed and his problems of a day or a year; and then only, and from this biased point of view, we have looked outward at the earth he has inhabited so briefly and at the universe in which our earth is so minute a part. Yet these are the great realities, and against them, we see our human problems from a different perspective. Perhaps if we reversed the telescope and looked at man down these long vistas, we should find less time and inclination to plan for our own destruction.' [157]

Other Books by the Author

Building Resilient Futures

ISBN: 9781035812622

Whether a community struggling to keep its members buoyant, a business trying to stay solvent, or a nation fighting to protect its citizens, adversity and crisis impact us all. The resilient are able to pick themselves up, dust themselves off, and not only bounce back but also bounce forward.

This book looks at what resilience means at times of crisis as well as the in-between periods. It examines the various types of resilience, such as emotional, organisational and societal, and offers valuable insights on how to manage the consequences of upheaval and trauma.

The author brings together contributors to deliver a real mix of theory, case study evidence and anecdote in a way that is both approachable and thought-provoking. It is a timely and necessary addition to a crucial topic. Very simply, professionals, practitioners, students, government ministers, and business leaders should read this now. It might be a safer, better world if people read the book and acted on it.

'A brilliant summary of the enormous challenges of gaining the ultimate resilience. Hugely entertaining and challenging. Very simply, professionals, practitioners, students, government ministers, and business leader should read this now. A safer, better world? … it might be if people read the book and act on it.'

'… the author has found a way to integrate the complexities necessary for businesses and organisations to achieve resilience. It is critical reading for all those who hold responsibility for organisational resilience.'

For orders, together with a sample and reviews, see: *https://www.austinmacauley.com/book/building-resilient-futures*

The Triptych

ISBN: 9781035830169

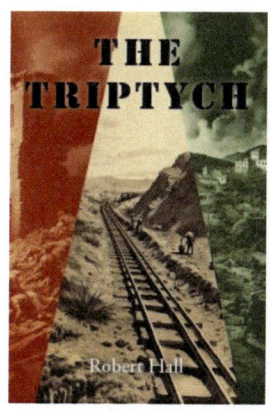

This is the story of three remarkable men. They were neither supreme sportsmen nor medical pioneers, with no fortunes or titles. Rather, they were ordinary men caught up in three periods of British history—the 1855 Siege of Sebastopol in the Crimean War, the expedition to rescue General Gordon in 1884–85, and the fierce Dodecanese Campaign in 1943. The prominence of the characters comes from the fact that all three survived their ordeals to reflect the spirit and resilience of their time. An old Russian triptych links the men's fortunes in this exciting novel.

This book is about our mindset to be better citizens and communities. While resilience is the central theme, it is a journey of discovery to learn more about the essence, philosophy and culture that supports our efforts to become more resilient. Resilience is itself a journey as there is no destination or final goal. One cannot become fully resilient as change is constantly happening to present new dilemmas and challenges. We need to adopt new ways of thinking to cope, and this book looks at past and present ideas.

For orders, see:
https://www.austinmacauley.com/book/the-triptych

The Resilience Mindset:
A Philosophical Journey

ISBN 9781035878284

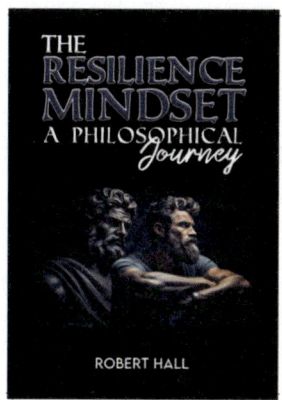

Resilience, whether professional or personal, requires not just practical measures but also a mindset or set of beliefs to be effective. That mindset is shaped by values, attitudes, culture, responsibilities and experience. These characteristics mould the way we incorporate new knowledge and how we make sense of the world and our place in it.

The Resilience Mindset takes a deep dive into the human aspects that lie behind resilience. It examines such topics as being stoical, facing our fears, realizing our virtues, finding our values, seeking truth and trust, and coping with change. Based on a philosophical journey throughout history, it provides valuable lessons for dealing with today's crises and challenges.

'… a valuable primer and stimulus to those who want to think deeply about the competences we should expect in our resilience leaders, and how those should be reflected in their selection, training and assessment.' *Bruce Mann, former Director of the UK's Civil Contingency Secretariat*

'The author blows away the myth that resilience is a modern phenomenon and examines the concept from the ancients to today. Intellectually stimulating and challenging.' *Richard Barnes, former Statutory Deputy Mayor of London*

For orders, see https://www.austinmacauley.com/book/the-resilience-mindset

References

Preface

[1] Hall, R. (2023) *Building Resilient Futures*, Austin Macauley. ISBN: 9781035812622. *https://www.austinmacauley.com/book/building-resilient-futures*

Foreword

[2] Oliver, T. (2020) *The Self Delusion: The Surprising Science of our Connection to Each Other and the Natural World*, W&N. ISBN: 1474611745. *https://www.weidenfeldandnicolson.co.uk/titles/tom-oliver/the-selfdelusion/9781474611763/*

Introduction

[3] Alexander, D. E. (2013) 'Resilience and disaster risk reduction: an etymological journey', *Natural Hazards and Earth System Sciences*, 13, 2707–2716.

https://nhess.copernicus.org/articles/13/2707/2013/nhess-13-2707-2013.html

[4] IPBES Global Assessment Preview (2019). *https://www.ipbes.net/news/ipbes-global-assessment-preview*

[5] Cornford, R., Spooner, S., McRaer, L., Purvis, A., Freeman, R. (2023) 'Ongoing overexploitation and delayed responses to environmental change highlight the urgency for action to promote vertebrate recoveries by 2030', *Proceedings of the Royal Society B.* *https://doi.org/10.1098/rspb.2023.0464*

[6] The Global Risk Report (2020) World Economic Forum. *https://www3.weforum.org/docs/WEF_Global_Risk_Report_2020.pdf*

[7] Kunming-Montreal Global Biodiversity Framework (2022) *https://www.cbd.int/doc/decisions/cop-15/cop-15-dec-04-en.pdf*

[8] Milo, R., Greenspoon, L., Krieger, E., Sender, R. (2023) 'The global biomass of wild mammals', *Proceedings of the National Academy of Science of the United States.* *https://www.pnas.org/doi/10.1073/pnas.2204892120*

[9] Earth Overshoot Day. *https://overshoot.footprintnetwork.org/*

[10] Holling, C. S. (1973) 'Resilience and stability of ecological systems', *Annual Review of Ecology and Systematics*, 4, 1–23. *https://www.annualreviews.org/content/journals/10.1146/annurev.es.04.110173.000245*

[11] Ibid, p. 14.

[12] Odum, E. P. (1985) 'Trends expected in stressed ecosystems', *BioScience*, 35, 7, 419–422.

[13] Odum, H. T. (1988) 'Self-organization, transformity, and information', *Science*, 242, 4882, 1132–1139.

[14] Sundt, P. (2010) 'Conceptual pitfalls and rangeland resilience', *Rangelands*, 32, 30–33.
https://scholar.google.co.uk/scholar?q=Sundt,+P.+Conceptu al+pitfalls+and+rangel and+resilience,+Rangelands,32,+30%E2%80%9333,+2010 .&hl=en&as_sdt=0&as_ vis=1&oi=scholart

[15] Oliver, T. H., et al. (2016) 'A synthesis is emerging between biodiversity-ecosystem function and ecological resilience research: reply to Mori', *Trends in Ecology and Evolution*, 31.
https://pubmed.ncbi.nlm.nih.gov/26774554/

[16] Oliver, T. H., et al. (2015) 'Biodiversity and resilience of ecosystem functions', *Trends in Ecology and Evolution*, 30, 11.
https://pubmed.ncbi.nlm.nih.gov/26437633/

[17] Armstrong, K. (2022) *Sacred Nature: How We Can Recover Our Bond with the Natural World*, Vintage Publishing. ISBN: 9781847926883.

[18] Lan G., et al. (2016) 'Why we need resilience thinking to meet societal challenges in bio-based production systems', *Current Opinion in Environmental Sustainability*, 23, 17–27.
https://www.sciencedirect.com/science/article/abs/pii/S1877 343516300884

[19] Weitzman, M. L., Metrick, A. (1998) 'Conflicts and choices in biodiversity preservation', *Journal of Economic Perspectives*, 12, 3, 21–34.
https://www.nsf.gov/news/how-do-microscopic-creatures-called-tardigrades#:~:text=Thomas%20Boothby%2C%20a%20Wyoming%20molecular,in%20the%20journal%20Communications%20Biology%20.

[20] Miller, W. R. (2011) 'Tardigrades', *American Scientist*, 99, 5. *https://www.americanscientist.org/article/tardigrades*

[21] US National Science Foundation (2022) 'How do microscopic creatures called tardigrades survive being completely dried out? Research News.
https://www.nsf.gov/news/how-do-microscopic-creatures-called-tardigrades

[22] Miller, W. R. Ibid.

[23] Chavez, C., Cruz-Becerra, G., Fei, J., Kassavetis. G. A., Kadonaga, J. T. (2019) 'The tardigrade damage suppressor protein binds to nucleosomes and protects DNA from hydroxyl radicals', *eLife.*
https://pubmed.ncbi.nlm.nih.gov/31571581/#:~:text=The%20tardigrade%20Ramaz zottius%20varieornatus%20contains,treatment%2C%20that%20generate%20hydr oxyl%20radicals.

[24] Babu, S. (2018) 'R-strategists, K-strategists and Survivorship curves: The reproductive adaptations of different organisms', *Eco-Intelligent.*
https://ecointelligent.com/2018/07/30/r-strategists-k-

strategists-and-survivorship-curves-thereproductive-
adaptions-of-different-organisms/comment-page-1/

[25] Schulze-Makuch, D. (2018) 'Turn up the heat: bacterial spores can take temperatures in the hundreds of degrees', *Smithsonian Magazine.*
https://www.smithsonianmag.com/air-space-magazine/turn-heat-bacterialspores-can-take-temperatures-hundreds-degrees-180970425/

[26] Biological Miracle (2022) National Park & Preserve Alaska. *https://www.nps.gov/gaar/learn/nature/wood-frog-page-2.htm*

[27] Ibid.

[28] Cano, R., Borucki, M. (1995) 'Revival and identification of bacterial spores in 25- to 40-million-year-old Dominican amber', *Science*, 268, 1060–1064.
https://www.science.org/doi/10.1126/science.7538699

[29] Shen-Miller, J. (2002) 'Sacred lotus, the long-living fruits of China antique', *Seed Science Research*, 12, 3, 131–143.
https://www.cambridge.org/core/journals/seed-science-research/article/abs/sacredlotus-the-longliving-fruits-of-china-antique/950DD5CB3E32BA6D99A79CAB5D75B038

[30] Shatilovich, A., et al. (2023) 'A novel nematode species from the Siberian permafrost shares adaptive mechanisms for cryptobiotic survival with *C. elegans* dauer larva', *PLOS Genetics*, 19, 7.
https://journals.plos.org/plosgeneicstics/article?id=10.1371/journal.pgen.1010798

[31] Whaley, D., Damyar, K., Witek, R. P., Mendoza, A., Alexander, M., Lakey, J. R. T. (2021) 'Cryopreservation: An

overview of principles and cell-specific considerations', *Cell Transplantation*, 30.
https://www.ncbi.nlm.nih.gov/pmc/articles/PMC7995302/
[32] Doyle, J. C., Alderson, D. L., Li, L., Low, S., Roughan, M., Shalunov, S., Tanaka, R., Willinger, W. (2005) 'The "robust yet fragile" nature of the Internet', Proceedings of National Academy of Sciences USA, 102, 41, 14497–502.
https://pubmed.ncbi.nlm.nih.gov/16204384/

Chapter 1

[33] Dizikes, P. (2011) 'When the butterfly effect took flight', *MIT News Magazine*.
https://www.technologyreview.com/2011/02/22/196987/when-the-butterfly-effect-took-flight/
[34] Taleb, N. N. (2012) *Antifragile: Things That Gain from Disorder*. ISBN: 0141038225.
[35] Manchester Arena Inquiry (2023) 'Radicalisation and preventability', Volume 3: Paragraph 24.132.
https://assets.publishing.service.gov.uk/media/63ff865ae90e0740dc92d1d8/MAI_Final_PDF_Volume_3.pdf
[36] Albaladejo-Robles, G., Böhm, M., Newbold, T. (2022) 'Species life-history strategies affect population responses to temperature and land-cover changes', *Global Change Biology*, 29, 1, 97–109.
https://onlinelibrary.wiley.com/doi/full/10.1111/gcb.16454
[37] Olsson, L., Rugbjerb, P., Pianale, L. T., Trivellin, C. (2022) 'Robustness: linking strain design to viable

bioprocesses', *Trends in Biotechnology*, 40, 8, 918–931.
https://pubmed.ncbi.nlm.nih.gov/35120750/

Chapter 2

[38] Cutajar, T. (2019) 'Who's eating Cane Toads and getting away with it?' Australian Museum.
https://australian.museum/blog/amri-news/whos_eating_cane_to_ads/
[39] Paul, L. R., Chapman, B. K., Chanway, C. P. (2002) 'Nitrogen fixation associated with *Suillus tomentosus* tuberculate ectomycorrhizae on *Pinus contorta* var. *latifolia*', *Annals of Botany*, 99, 6, 1101–1109.
https://www.ncbi.nlm.nih.gov/pmc/articles/PMC3243579/
[40] Tyrrell, K. A. (2019) 'Resilience of Yellowstone's forests tested by unprecedented fire, University of Wisconsin-Madison'.
https://news.wisc.edu/resilience-of-yellowstones-forests-tested-by-unprecedented-fire/
[41] Rudolf, J. C. 'Climate change takes toll on the lodgepole pine', *The New York Times*.
https://archive.nytimes.com/green.blogs.nytimes.com/2011/0 2/28/climate-change-takes-toll-on-the-lodgepole-pine/
[42] Cook, S. P., Carroll, A. D., Limsey, M., Shaw, T. M. (2015) 'Changes in a primary resistance parameter of lodgepole pine to bark beetle attack one year following fertilization and thinning', *Forests*, 6, 2, 280–292.
https://www.mdpi.com/1999-4907/6/2/280#B14-forests-06-00280

[43] Ruff, C., Holt, B., Trinkaus, E. (2006) 'Who's afraid of the big bad Wolff? "Wolff's law" and bone functional adaptation', *American Journal of Physical Anthropology*, 129, 4.

[44] Ackerman, J. (2012) 'How bacteria in our bodies protect our health', *Scientific American*. *https://www.scientificamerican.com/article/ultimate-social-network-bacteria-protects-health/*

[45] Human Microbiome Project defines normal bacterial makeup of the body (2012) National Institutes of Health. *https://www.nih.gov/news-events/news-releases/nih-human-microbiome-project-defines-normal-bacterial-makeup-body*

[46] Ackerman, J. Ibid.

[47] Offord, C. (2023) 'Microbe stops mosquitoes from harboring malaria parasite', *Science*. *https://enterprisewired.com/mosquitoes-from-harboring-malaria-parasite/*

[48] Trotter, W. (2013) *The Winter War: The Russo-Finnish War of 1939–40*, Arum Press. ISBN: 185410933.

Chapter 3

[49] Sagarin, R. (2012) *Learning from the Octopus. How Secrets from Nature Can Help Us Fight Terrorist Attacks, Natural Disasters and Disease*, Basic Books. ISBN: 9780465021833.

[50] Wagh, M. (2022) The strange mechanics of fire ant rafts, *Popular Mechanics*.

https://www.popularmechanics.com/science/animals/a41244217/mechanics-of-fire-ant-rafts/

[51] Ko, H., Komilian, K., Waters, J. S., Hu, D. L. (2022) Metabolic scaling of fire ants (*Solenopsis invicta*) engaged in collective behaviors', *Biology Open*, 11, 2. *https://www.ncbi.nlm.nih.gov/pmc/articles/PMC8905630/*

[52] Staying above water: A systemic response to rising flood risk (2023) MarshMcLennan. *https://www.marshmclennan.com/insights/publications/2023/february/staying-above-water-a-systemic-response-to-rising-flood-risk.html*

[53] Guy Carpenter's Recent Insights on Flood Risk and Solutions (2023). *https://www.guycarp.com/insights/2023/03/guy-carpenter-spotlights-flood-insurance-content.html*

[54] 'Bangladesh's riverine villages are benefiting from clever design' (2023) *The Economist*.

[55] Pedroso, M. (2019) Blind co-operation: The evolution of redundancy via ignorance, philosophy and religious studies, Towson University (USA). *https://philpapers.org/rec/PEDBCT-2*

[56] Schmidt, J. O. (2019) 'Pain and lethality induced by insect stings: An exploratory and correlational study', *Toxins (Basel)*, 11, 7, 427. *https://www.ncbi.nlm.nih.gov/pmc/articles/PMC6669698/*

[57] Zolli, A., Healy, A. M. (2012) *Resilience: Why Things Bounce Back*, Headline Publishing. ISBN: 9780755360352.

[58] Meadows, D. (2008) *Thinking in Systems: A Primer*. ISBN: 10:1603580557.

Chapter 4

[59] Gonzales-Bernardo, W., Russo, L. F., Valderrabano, E., Fernandez, A., Penteriani, V. (2020) 'Denning in brown bears', *Ecology and Evolution*, 10, 13, 6844–6862. *https://www.ncbi.nlm.nih.gov/pmc/articles/PMC7381752/*

[60] Barnes, B. M. (1989) 'Freeze avoidance in a mammal: body temperatures below 0°C in an Arctic hibernator', *Science*, 244, 1521–1616. *https://pubmed.ncbi.nlm.nih.gov/2740905/*

[61] Mesa, N. (2023) 'Hibernating bears provide clue to preventing serious clots in humans', *The Scientist*. *https://www.the-scientist.com/hibernating-bears-provide-clue-to-preventing-serious-clots-in-humans-71064*

[62] White, I. (2020) 'How and why hazel dormice hibernate', People's Trust for Endangered Species. *https://ptes.org/how-and-why-hazel-dormice-hibernate/*

[63] Combe, F., Juŝkaitis, R., Trout, R. C., Ellis, J. S., Norrey, J., AL-Fulaij, N., White, I., Harris, W. E. (2022) 'Density and climate effects on age-specific survival and population growth: consequences for hibernating mammals', *Animal Conservation*, 26, 3, 317–330. *https://zslpublications.onlinelibrary.wiley.com/doi/10.1111/acv.12843*

[64] Yang, Y., Yuan, J., Field, R. L., Ye, D., Hu, Z., Xu, K., Xu, L., Gong, Y., Yue, Y., Kravitz, A. V., Bruchas, M. R., Cui, J., Brestoff, J. R., Chen, H. (2023) 'Induction of a torporlike hypothermic and hypometabolic state in rodents by

ultrasound', *Nature Metabolism*.
https://www.nature.com/articles/s42255-023-00804-z

[65] World Economic Forum (2023) The Global Risks Report, 18th Edition.
https://www3.weforum.org/docs/WEF_Global_Risks_Report_2023.pdf

[66] Mitigation Saves up to $13 per $1 Invested. (2020) National Institute of Building Sciences.
https://www.nibs.org/files/pdfs/ms_v4_overview.pdf

Chapter 5

[67] Finn, J., Tregenza, T., Norman, M. (2009) 'Defensive tool use in a coconut-carrying octopus', *Current Biology*, 19, 23.
https://www.sciencedirectcom/science/article/pii/S0960982209019149

[68] Godfrey-Smith, P. (2017) 'The mind of an octopus', *Scientific American*.
https://www.scientificamerican.com/article/the-mind-of-an-octopus/

[69] Godfrey-Smith, P. (2017) *Other Minds: The Octopus, the Sea, and the Deep Origins of Consciousness*, HarperCollins. ISBN: 9780008226299.

[70] Devereux, C. (2021) 'Cruelty claim as world's first octopus farm poised to open in Spain', *The Times*.

[71] Nield, N. (2018) 'Biologists have discovered an underwater octopus city and they're calling it octlantis', *Nature. https://www.sciencealert.com/marine-biologists-*

discover-an-underwater-octopus-city-octlantis-jervis-bay-australia

[72] Barry, J. P., Litvin, S. Y, Devogelaere, A., Caress, D. W., Martin, E. J. (2023) 'Abyssal hydrothermal springs–Cryptic incubators for brooding octopus', *Science Advances*, 9, 34. *https://www.science.org/doi/10.1126/sciadv.adg3247*

[73] Lesté-Lasserre, C. (2023) 'Animals that are social outliers seem to be better at solving problems', *New Scientist*. *https://www.newscientist.com/article/2367828-animals-that-are-social-outliersseem-to-be-better-at-solving-problems/*

[74] Hendry, L. Octopuses keep surprising us–here are eight examples how, National History Museum. *https://www.nhm.ac.uk/discover/octopuses-keep-surprising-us-here-are-eight-examples-how.html*

[75] Heimbuch, J. (2021) '7 Clever behaviors of octopuses', *Treehugger*. *https://www.treehugger.com/astounding-behaviors-of-octopuses-4863780*

[76] Bielecki, J., Dam Nielsen, S. K., Nachman, G., Garm, A. (2023) 'Associative learning in the box jellyfish *Tripedalia cystophora*', *Current Biology*. *https://pubmed.ncbi.nlm.nih.gov/37741280/*

[77] Brende, B., Sternfels, B. (2023) 'Seizing the momentum to build resilience for a future of sustainable inclusive growth', McKinsey and Company. *https://www.mckinsey.com/capabilities/risk-and-resilience/our-insights/seizing-themomentum-to-build-resilience-for-a-future-of-sustainable-inclusive-growth*

[78] Sagarin, R. Ibid.

Chapter 6

[79] Wohlleben, P. (2016) *The Hidden Life of Trees: What They Feel, How They Communicate-Discoveries from a Secret World*. ISBN: 1771642483

[80] *The Times of Israel* (2023). *https://www.timesofisrael.com/ingroundbreaking-research-tel-aviv-u-team-records-plants-talking-for-first-time/*

[81] Figueiredo, A., Boy, J., Guggenberger, G. (2021) 'Common mycorrhizae network: a review of the theories and mechanisms behind underground interactions', *Fungal Biology*. *https://www.frontiersin.org/journals/fungal-biology/articles/10.3389/ffunb.2021.735299/full*

[82] Interview with Suzanne Simard (2021) *New Scientist*. *https://www.newscientist.com/article/mg25033320-900-suzanne-simard-interviewhow-i-uncovered-the-hidden-language-of-trees/*

[83] Marschner, H., Dell, B. (1994) 'Nutrient uptake in mycorrhizal symbiosis', *Plant and Soil*, 159, 1. *https://link.springer.com/article/10.1007/BF00000098*

[84] Mbodj, D., Effa-Effa, B., Kane, A., Manneh, B., Gantet, P., Laplaze, L., Diedhiou, A. G., Grondin, A. (2018) 'Arbuscular mycorrhizal symbiosis in rice: Establishment, environmental control and impact on plant growth and resistance to abiotic stresses', *Rhizosphere*, 8, 12–26. *https://www.sciencedirect.com/science/article/abs/pii/S2452 21981830079X*

[85] Simard, S., Perry, D. A., Smith, J., Molina, R. (2008) 'Effects of soil trenching on occurrence of ectomycorrhizas on *Pseudotsuga menziesii* seedlings grown in mature forests of *Betula papyrifera* and *Pseudotsuga menziesii*', *New Phytologist*.
https://nph.onlinelibrary.wiley.com/doi/10.1046/j.1469-8137.1997.00731.x

[86] Dickie, I. A., Koide, R. T., Steiner, K. C. (2002) 'Influences of established trees on mycorrhizas, nutrition and growth of *Quercus rubra* seedlings', *Ecological Monographs*, 72, 4, 505–521.
https://www.researchgate.net/publication/201997135_Influences_of_Established_Trees_on_Mycorrhizas_Nutrition_and_Growth_of_Quercus_rubra_Seedlings

[87] Hug That Tree—It May Be Crying: New Evidence Shakes Up Science (2023) WoodCentral.
https://woodcentral.com.au/hug-that-tree-it-may-becrying-new-evidence-shakes-up-science/

[88] Marris, E. (2023) 'Stressed plants 'cry' and some animals can probably hear them', *Scientific American*.
https://www.scientificamerican.com/article/stressed-plants-cry-and-some-animalscan-probably-hear-them/

[89] Khait, I., et al. 'Sounds emitted by plants under stress are airborne and informative', *Cell Press*, 186, 1328–1336.
https://www.cell.com/cell/pdf/S0092-8674(23)00262-3.pdf

[90] The secret language of trees, Zambezi Grande.
https://www.zambezigrande.com/uncategorized/the-secret-language-of-trees/

[91] Van Der Heijden, M. G., Horton, T. R. (2009) 'Socialism in soil? The importance of mycorrhizal fungal networks for facilitation in natural ecosystems', *Journal of Ecology*, 97, 1139–1150.
https://besjournals.onlinelibrary.wiley.com/doi/10.1111/j.136 5-2745.2009.01570.x

[92] AntWiki, Supercolonies,
https://www.antwiki.org/wiki/Supercolonies

[93] Sosa, S., Jacoby, D. M. P., Lihoreau, M., Sueur, C. (2021) 'Animal social networks: Towards an integrative framework embedding social interactions, space and time', *Methods in Ecology and Evolution*.
https://besjournals.onlinelibrary.wiley.com/doi/10.1111/2041 -210X.13539

[94] 'The importance of networking in community development'. (2021) Zapnito.
https://knowledge.zapnito.com/posts/the-importance-of-networking-in-community-development

[95] Staughton, J. (2022) 'What are holobionts?' *ScienceABC*.
https://www.scienceabc.com/pure-sciences/what-are-holobionts.html

Chapter 7

[96] Wahl, D. C. (2017) 'What exactly are resilience and transformative resilience?' *Medium*.
https://designforsustainability.medium.com/what-exactly-areresilience-and-transformative-resilience-a0783595023f

[97] Olsson, P., Folke, C., Hahn, T. (2004) 'Social-ecological transformation for ecosystem management: the development of adaptive co-management of a wetland landscape in Southern Sweden', *Ecology and Society*, 9, 4. *http://www.ecologyandsociety.org/vol9/iss4/art2/*

[98] 'What is business transformation?' (2023) McKinsey & Company. *https://www.mckinsey.com/featured-insights/mckinsey-explainers/what-is-business-transformation*

[99] Jabr, F. (2012) 'How does a caterpillar turn into a butterfly?' *Scientific American*. *https://www.scientificamerican.com/article/caterpillar-butterfly-metamorphosis-explainer/*

[100] Magulis, L., Sagan, D. (2008) *Acquiring Genomes: A Theory of the Origin of Species*, Basic Books. ASIN: B06XC9FBX1.

[101] Cuginotti, A. Imaginal Cells | The Caterpillar's Job to Resist the Butterfly. *https://augustocuginotti.com/imaginal-cells-caterpillars-job-to-resist-butterfly/*

[102] Dichter, S. F., Gagnon, C., Alexander, A. (1993) 'Leading organizational transformations', McKinsey & Company. *https://www.mckinsey.com/capabilities/people-and-organizationalperformance/our-insights/leading-organizational-transformations*

[103] 'What is digital transformation?' (2023) McKinsey & Company. *https://www.mckinsey.com/featured-insights/mckinsey-explainers/what-is-digital-transformation*

[104] High Line. *https://en.wikipedia.org/wiki/High_Line*

[105] High Line. *https://www.thehighline.org/gardens/*

[106] Verburg, R., Rahn, E., Verweij, P., van Kuijk, M., Ghazoul, J. (2019) 'An innovation perspective to climate change adaptation in coffee systems', *Environmental Science & Policy*, 97, 16–24. *https://www.sciencedirect.com/science/article/pii/S1462901119301777*

[107] Biddle, S. (2023) 'Back in the trenches: Why new technology hasn't revolutionized warfare in Ukraine', *Foreign Affairs*. *https://www.foreignaffairs.com/ukraine/back-trenches-technology-warfare*

Chapter 8

[108] Planes, S., Allemand, D. (2023) 'Insights and achievements from the Tara Pacific expedition', *Nature Communications*, 14, 3131. *https://www.nature.com/articles/s41467-023-38896-6*

[109] Evans, L. The Morphology of Limpet Species on the Rocky Shore of Lundy, Report of Lundy Field Society, 48. *https://lfs-resources.s3.amazonaws.com/ar48/LFS_Annual_Report_Vol_48_Part_18.pdf*

[110] Hall, R. (1972) 'The relationship between radula length and position on the shore in the Common Limpet', Thesis Paper (unpublished), University of Bristol.

[111] Barber, A. H., Lu, D. F., Pugno, N. M. (2015) 'Extreme strength observed in limpet teeth', *Journal of the Royal Society*, 12, 105.

https://royalsocietypublishing.org/doi/10.1098/rsif.2014.132 6

[112] Harley, C. D. G., Denny, M. W., Mach, K. J., Miller, L. P. (2009) 'Thermal stress and morphological adaptations in limpets', *Functional Ecology*, 23, 2, 292–301. *https://www.researchgate.net/publication/228007134_Therm al_stress_and_morphological_adaptations_in_limpets*

[113] Energy Saver, Cool Roofs. *https://www.energy.gov/energysaver/cool-roofs*

[114] Using Green Roofs to Reduce Heat Islands, US Environmental Protection Agency. *https://www.epa.gov/heatislands/using-green-roofs-reduce-heat-islands*

[115] How coral reefs can survive climate change (2023) ScienceDaily. www.sciencedaily.com/releases/2023/06/230626163854.htm

[116] Fedele, G., Donatti, C. I., Harvey, C. A., Hannah, L., Hole, D. G. (2019) 'Transformative adaptation to climate change for sustainable social-ecological systems', *Environmental Science & Policy*, 101, 116–125. *https://www.sciencedirect.com/science/article/pii/S14629011 19305337*

[117] Ibid.

[118] Clunk Click Every Trip. *https://en.wikipedia.org/wiki/Clunk_Click_Every_Trip*

Chapter 9

[119] Sagarin, R. Ibid.

[120] Hanson, B., Lindblom, S. D., Loeffler, M. L., Pilon-Smits, E. A. H. (2004) 'Selenium protects plants from phloem-feeding aphids due to both deterrence and toxicity', *New Phytologist*, 162, 655–662.
https://nph.onlinelibrary.wiley.com/doi/10.1111/j.1469-8137.2004.01067.x

[121] Brooks, J. (2018) 'Coloration, camouflage, and sexual dichromatism in the Northern Pacific rattlesnake (*Crotalus oreganus*)', All Master's Thesis, 957.
https://digitalcommons.cwu.edu/etd/957/

[122] Allf, B. C., Durst, P. A. P., Pfennig, D. W. (2016) 'Behavioural plasticity and the origins of novelty: The evolution of the rattlesnake rattle', *The American Naturalist*, 188, 4.
https://www.researchgate.net/publication/305720035_Behav ioral_Plasticity_and_th
e_Origins_of_Novelty_The_Evolution_of_the_Rattlesnake_ Rattle#pf2

[123] Osipov, A., Utkin, Y. (2023) 'What are the neurotoxins in hemotoxic snake venoms?' *International Journal of Molecular Science*, 24, 3, 2919.
https://pmc.ncbi.nlm.nih.gov/articles/PMC9917609/

[124] Rolan, T. D. (2015) 'Neurotoxic snakes of the Americas', *Neurology Clinical Practice*, 5, 5, 383–388.
https://www.ncbi.nlm.nih.gov/pmc/articles/PMC5762023/

[125] Cornish, P. (2022) 'Rediscovering deterrence', Essay no. 1: 'What is strategic deterrence and why does it matter?' CityForum

[126] Better camouflage is needed to hide from new electronic sensors (2023) *The Economist.*

[127] Gottemoeller, R. (2023) 'Russian attacks would be far worse without NATO's "proximity" deterrence', *The Economist.*

[128] Sagarin, R. Ibid.

Chapter 10

[129] Quamber-Hill, S. (2023) 'Resilience first response to climate champions on COP15: Biodiversity summit', *Resilience First. https://resiliencefirst.org/news/resilience-first-response-to-climate-champions-on-cop15-biodiversity-summit/*

[130] The Climate Resilient Infrastructure Report, Issue 2, 2023. *https://sustainability-coalition.org/publication/the-climate-resilience-infrastructure-report-a-focus-on-nature/*

[131] Rewilding Britain. *https://www.rewildingbritain.org.uk/why-rewild/benefits-of-rewilding/why-we-need-rewilding*

[132] Rewilding boosts jobs and volunteering, study, Rewilding Britain, 9 March 2021. *https://www.rewildingbritain.org.uk/press-hub/rewilding-boosts-jobs-and-volunteering-opportunities-study-shows*

[133] The TNFD Nature-related Risk and Opportunity Management and Disclosure Framework Final Draft. (2023). *https://tnfd.global/wp-content/uploads/2023/07/TNFD-Framework-Summary-Executive-Summary-Beta-v0-2-1.pdf?v=1690527779*

[134] Empowering companies and cities for credible nature action. (2024) Science Based Targets Network *https://sciencebasedtargetsnetwork.org/*

[135] Nature and net zero, World Economic Forum 2021. *https://www.weforum.org/reports/nature-and-net-zero/*

[136] Ibid.

[137] 'Enfield's baby beaver is another first for London', Enfield Council newsletter, 28 September 2023. *https://www.enfield.gov.uk/news-and-events/2023/09/enfields-baby-beaver-is-another-first-for-london*

[138] Rewilding Britain, What's so special about beavers? *https://www.rewildingbritain.org.uk/why-rewild/reintroductions-key-species/reintroductions-and-bringing-back-species/whats-so-special-about-beavers*

[139] Ronnquist, A. L., Westbrook, C. J. (2021) 'Beaver dams: How structure, flow state, and landscape setting regulate water storage and release', *Science of the Total Environment*, 785. *https://www.sciencedirect.com/science/article/abs/pii/S0048969721024049*

[140] Graf, P. M., Wilson, R. P., Sanchez, L. C., Hacklander, K., Rosell, F. (2018) 'Diving behavior in a free-living, semi-aquatic herbivore, the Eurasian beaver *Castor fiber*', *Ecology and Evolution*, 8, 2, 997–1008. *https://openarchive.usn.no/usn-xmlui/handle/11250/2486685*

[141] Wright, J. P., Jones, C. G., Flecker, A. S. (2002) 'An ecosystem engineer, the beaver, increases species richness at

the landscape scale', *Oecologia*, 132, 96–101.
https://link.springer.com/article/10.1007/s00442-002-0929-1

[142] McKinstry, M. C., Caffrey, P., Anderson, S. H. (2001) 'The importance of beavers to waterfowl and wetlands habitats in Wyoming', *Journal of the American Water Resources Association*, 37, 6, 1571–1577. *https://onlinelibrary.wiley.com/doi/10.1111/j.1752-1688.2001.tb03660.x*

[143] Luedke, H. (2019) 'Fact sheet | Nature as resilient infrastructure—An overview of nature-based solutions', Environmental and Energy Study Institute. *https://www.eesi.org/papers/view/fact-sheet-nature-as-resilient-infrastructure-an-overview-of-nature-based-solutions*

[144] Schoettle, A. W., Jacobi, W. R., Waring, K. M., Burns, K. S. (2019) 'Regeneration for resilience framework to support regeneration decisions for species with populations at risk of extirpation by white pine blister rust', *New Forests*, 50, 89114. *https://www.researchgate.net/publication/327401744_Regeneration_for_resilience_framework_to_support_regeneration_decisions_for_species_with_populations_at_risk_of_extirpation_by_white_pine_blister_rust*

[145] Aldrich, D. P. (2012) 'Social capital in post disaster recovery: towards a resilient and compassionate East Asian community', in Sawada, Y. and S. Oum (eds.), Economic and Welfare Impacts of Disasters in East Asia and Policy Responses. ERIA Research Project Report 2011-8, Jakarta: ERIA. pp.157–178. *https://www.eria.org/Chapter_5.pdf*

Chapter 11

[146] 'The Future of Nature', WWF

[147] 2024 Living Planet Report, WWF.
https://livingplanet.panda.org/en-GB/

[148] A fifth of countries worldwide at risk from ecosystem collapse as biodiversity declines, reveals pioneering Swiss Re Index. 23 September 2020.
https://www.swissre.com/media/press-release/nr-20200923-biodiversity-and-ecosystems-services.html

[149] Burke, L., Reytar, K., Spalding, M., Perry, A. (2011) 'Reefs at risk revisited', World Resources Institute.
https://www.wri.org/research/reefs-risk-revisited

[150] Gallup Global Emotions report (2023).
https://www.gallup.com/analytics/349280/gallup-global-emotions-report.aspx

[151] Household income inequality, UK: financial year ending 2022, ONS.
https://www.ons.gov.uk/peoplepopulationandcommunity/personalandhouseholdfinances/incomeandwealth/bulletins/householdincomeinequalityfinancial/financialyearending2022

Epilogue

[152] Caulin, A. C., Maley, C. C. (2011) 'Peto's paradox: Evolution's prescription for cancer prevention', *Trends in Ecology and Evolution*, 26, 4, 175–182.
https://pubmed.ncbi.nlm.nih.gov/21296451/

[153] Vollrath, F. 'Uncoupling elephant TP53 and cancer', *Trends in Ecology and Evolution*, 38, 8, 705–707. *https://pubmed.ncbi.nlm.nih.gov/37385845/*

[154] Lin, Y. C., Sarica, G. M., Chua, T. J., Jenkins, S. F., Switzer, A. D., Woo, G., Lallemant, D. (2021) 'Asia's looming Black Elephant events', *Communications Earth & Environment.* *https://www.researchgate.net/publication/355146239_Asia's_looming_Black_Eleph ant_events*

[155] The futurist's metaphorical menagerie, 15 March 2020. *https://www.dayonefutures.nz/blog/2020/3/15/the-futurists-metaphorical-menagerie*

[156] Taleb, N. N. (2007) *The Black Swan: The Impact of the Highly Improbable*, Penguin. ISBN: 0141034599.

[157] Carson, R. (1952) 'Acceptance speech of the National Book Award for Non-fiction', Quoted in *The Maginalian.* *https://www.themarginalian.org/2022/11/30/rachel-carson-national-book-award-speech/*

Index

224